ULTIMATE PAPER AIRPLANES FOR KIDS

ANDREW DEWAR

TUTTLE Publishing

Tokyo | Rutland, Vermont | Singapore

Contents

The Planes

Belly Button 34

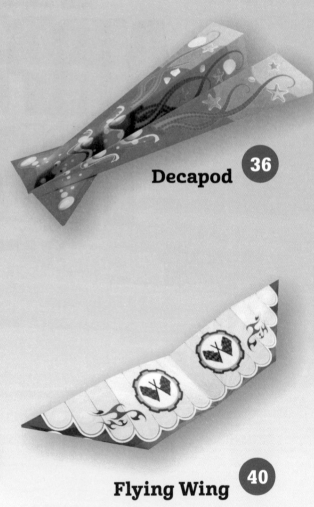

Decapod 36

Hammerhead 38

Flying Wing 40

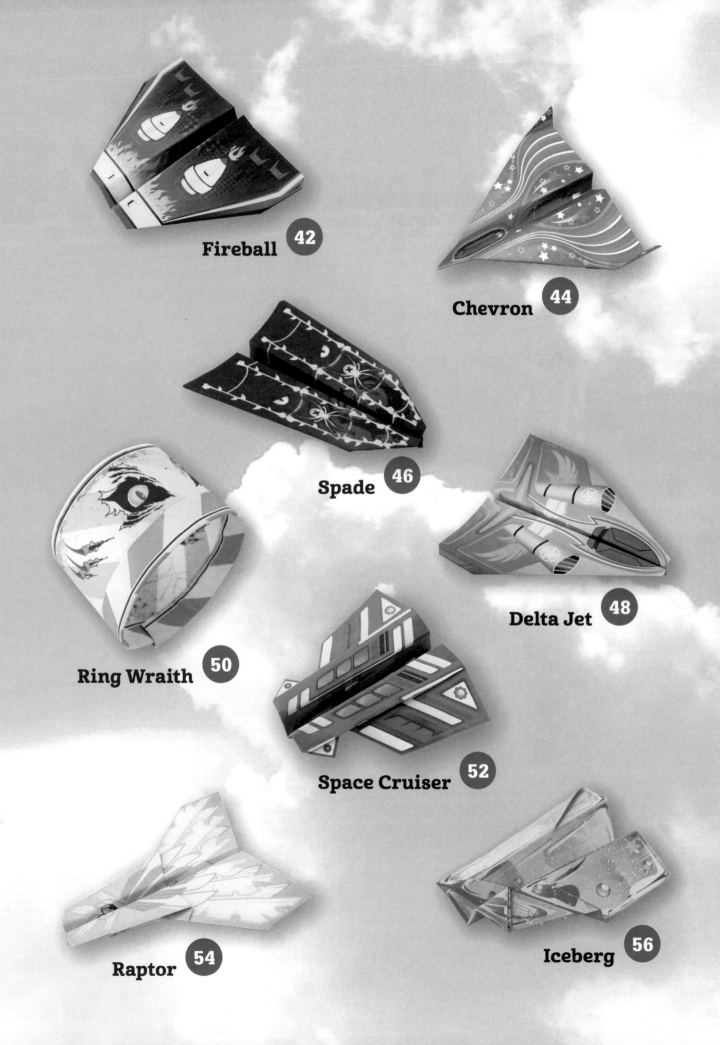

Fireball 42

Chevron 44

Spade 46

Delta Jet 48

Ring Wraith 50

Space Cruiser 52

Raptor 54

Iceberg 56

When I was a kid...

... I made paper airplanes constantly. I occasionally bought some balsa wood and tissue, a propeller, and a bit of rubber, and then spent several weekends turning these items into a model airplane. I knew from magazines that it should fly great, if I had the patience to build and trim it properly. What I really wanted to do was get out flying right away. Several days of building were too much for me. My balsa planes didn't fly.

But if I used paper instead of balsa, I found I could fold and test, refold and retest, come up with a decent model in a few hours, and be out on the lawn flying in no time. (And paper didn't require trips to a distant shop to buy special supplies!)

Even now that I'm a big kid, that sense of exhilaration I feel when a new airplane goes clear across the room and hits the far wall keeps me excited about folding new models.

The planes in this book are the ultimate expression of that desire for interesting planes that can be folded quickly but still have amazing performance. By carefully following the instructions and numbered lines on the paper, these planes can be assembled and trimmed in little more than a minute. Yet they fly for a surprisingly long time—probably longer than any origami airplane you've folded before! Models like the Delta Jet might even fly clear across the park!

Paper airplanes can glide a long way, down a long straight line, before hitting the ground. Or they can catch thermals and soar higher and higher, until finally they're gone from sight altogether.

It seems like magic, but it's not. With not much more than a piece of paper, you can make gliders that zip across the room or waft into the sky. This book will tell you how.

Why Planes Fly ... or Don't!

There are lots of ways that things can fly. They can be lighter than air, like a party balloon, and float on the breeze. They can be picked up by the wind, like a kite, or a spider, or a dandelion seed. They can rise on a jet of hot air or gas, like a rocket. They can flap their wings, like hummingbirds and bees. They can be pushed or pulled by an engine, like a jumbo jet. Or they can glide on wide-spread wings, like sailplanes, eagles, and paper airplanes.

But what do we mean when we talk about flying?

To be flying, an object has to stay in the air and not fall down. Some people might tell you that the best paper airplane, the one that goes farthest of all, is a tight wad of paper. But that isn't flying. The wad is falling from the moment it leaves your hand. To be flying, it has to keep going steadily, and not slow down or dive to the ground. Paper airplanes can't stay up forever, but they can glide a long way, down a long straight line, before hitting the ground.

This section will tell you how those wings of paper really fly.

Animals that Fly

Only four kinds of animals have ever learned how to truly fly: insects, birds, bats, and pterosaurs.

Insects are the oldest fliers. They have been flitting about for 300 million years or more. They flap specialized wings to get around. Pterosaurs, birds, and bats all turned their arms and hands into wings, and used flaps of skin or grew feathers to give them the big, wide shape they need to create lift. We humans can't fly because our arms and hands are best suited for holding tools, not grabbing the air!

Pterosaurs were like flying dinosaurs, and they are extinct now. That's probably a good thing, because the biggest ones were as big as a Cessna airplane!

Some people think pterosaurs survived until quite recently, and that's what legendary dragons really were. What do you think?

There are many other animals that can glide or parachute, like flying fish and flying squirrels, but they can't take off from the ground and they can't sustain themselves in the air. But they use fins, feet, stretched skin, or flattened bodies to create enough lift to slow their fall and travel forward. Some flying fish are such good gliders that they can skim more than 300 yards over the waves!

know what? Not everything with wings can glide. Only three kinds of insects can stay in the air without moving their wings. Which ones? Butterflies, dragonflies, and locusts. That's why butterflies can migrate thousands of miles. They can rest their wings while they glide. All the other insects have to flap frantically all the time. Whew!

Creating Lift

"Lift" is what holds flying things up. In an airplane, lift is made by the wing moving through the air. How? Let's find out!

PUSHING ALL THE TIME

Did you know that air is pushing on us all the time? Still air

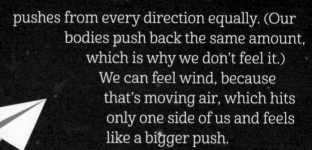

pushes from every direction equally. (Our bodies push back the same amount, which is why we don't feel it.) We can feel wind, because that's moving air, which hits only one side of us and feels like a bigger push.

A shape that is curved on top and flat on the bottom is ideal for a wing profile. It will create lift when air flows over it, because the air flows faster over the top, reducing the pressure pushing down on that surface. The greater pressure pushing on the bottom lifts it up. This kind of *cambered* (curved) shape is called an airfoil. Why does the air on the top of the wing speed up? And why does that lower the air pressure there? It's because of three special effects: the *Coanda Effect*, the *Kutta Condition*, and *Bernoulli's Principle*.

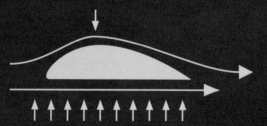 

Bernoulli's Principle says that the faster a fluid flows, the less pressure it exerts. So if the air on the top of the wing is going faster, there's less pressure pushing down. That means the higher pressure on the bottom of the wing pushes it up. And lift ensues!

The Coanda Effect says that fluids (like air and water) tend to stay attached to surfaces they flow over. This means that air follows the curve at the top of the wing. And because of the **Kutta Condition**, created by the sharp back edge of the airfoil, the air speeds up as it flows over the curve. It speeds up so much that it gets to the back of the wing faster than the air going under it!

KITES

Think about kites. They are a wing that stays in one place while wind moves over them. The wind wants to go in a straight line, so when a kite is in the way, the wind tries to push it aside, making it rise. This creates a lot of drag, too, which pushes the kite backwards at the same time. Without a string to hold it still, the kite would not be able to keep air moving over it. This is why

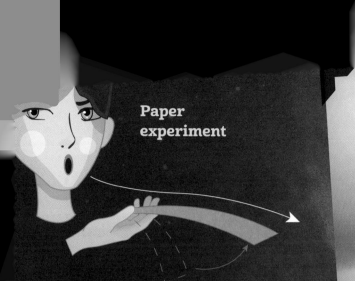

Paper experiment

Spoon experiment

TRY IT!

Here are two experiments you can try. First, blow over the top of a drooping sheet of paper. The paper will rise up and stand out straight, supported by the greater air pressure under it. Next, try touching a steady flow of tap water with the bottom of a spoon. You'd expect the spoon to be pushed away, but in fact it is pulled into the flow. That's because the speed of the water reduces the pressure on the bottom of the spoon, and air on the other side pushes it.

airplanes based on kites (and there were a lot of them at first!) usually failed.

The Wright brothers are famous for being the first to fly a powered airplane. But they had trouble at first. Their wings didn't work! They put test models on their bicycles and rode around, and then made a little wind tunnel to test more models. But they didn't know that small wings are different from big ones. The models that worked best were almost flat, but when they were turned into full-sized wings, they were too thin and hardly made any lift!

Making lift sounds simple, and it basically is. But lift doesn't just pull upward. Remember, air pushes in all directions, so lift is produced anywhere that pressure has been reduced. In airplane

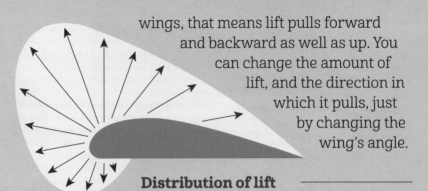

Distribution of lift

wings, that means lift pulls forward and backward as well as up. You can change the amount of lift, and the direction in which it pulls, just by changing the wing's angle.

ANGLE OF ATTACK

By increasing the angle of attack (the angle at which the wing hits the airflow) you can increase the amount of lift. Air going over the top of the wing has to go faster, and air striking the bottom creates more pressure (the kite principle). The bigger the angle, the more lift. But if the angle becomes too big, the Coanda Effect stops, and the air comes unstuck and gets turbulent. If that happens, the wing stops making lift and stalls. In other words, it stops flying.

More speed means more lift. But more lift is not necessarily better. Lift creates drag, which holds the wing and the airplane back. And drag increases much faster than the speed. When the airplane doubles its speed, the drag created by the wing quadruples! So more and more power is needed to go faster, in spite of the lift.

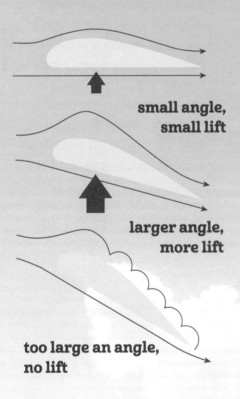

small angle, small lift

larger angle, more lift

too large an angle, no lift

know what? Sometimes people say you can feel lift and drag for yourself by putting your hand out the window of a moving car. It's true, but it isn't a safe thing to do. Instead, try putting your hand close to the hose of a vacuum cleaner. Does it suck your hand? That's because the air pressure is lower inside the vacuum, just like the top of a wing, and the thicker air outside is pushing your hand. Turn your hand sideways to the flow and then back to flat again. Feel the difference? That's drag.

Streamlining

THICK OR THIN?

Too many layers of paper folded up at the front make the wing too thick. Air can't go around it smoothly, so it gets unstuck and turbulent at the back. A thinner (or more sharply creased) wing is much better. By the way, putting thick folds on the top side of the wing doesn't work very well either!

It's important for an airplane to be streamlined. It has to be smooth and slick to slip through the air easily. Sleek looking airplanes fly fast because they cut right through the air. Wings and airfoils need to be streamlined too.

The more streamlined a wing is, the more easily air can move around it. A blunt plate is the worst. Not only does it practically stop the air, but the flow behind it is turbulent and messy. A half circle also makes turbulence, because the air can't join up neatly behind it. Round is better, and flat is most streamlined of all. But remember, flat wings don't make much lift either. So the best wing shape is the one with the least drag for the most lift. In paper airplanes, that is a thin wing with two or three layers at the front.

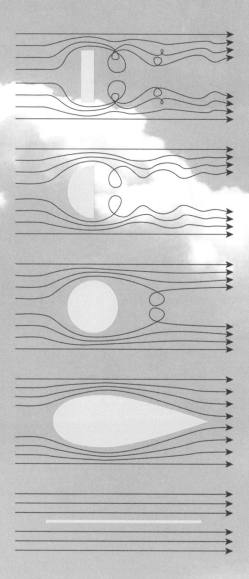

Balance...

No matter how amazing a plane looks, it won't fly unless it has balance. No amount of wishing will do. Here's why!

Say you have a plane which is just a wing and nothing else. The center of gravity, or place where it balances, is just about in the middle of the wing. But, depending on the shape of the airfoil, the center of lift, or place where the lift pulls it up, is a quarter or a third from the front edge. So what happens? The front edge pops up, and the wing twirls around and around. If you add some weight to the front of the wing so that the centers of lift and gravity are in the same place, the wing will balance and fly straight!

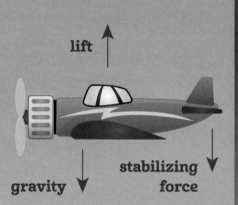

lift

gravity

stabilizing force

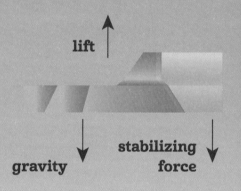

lift

gravity

stabilizing force

STABILIZING FORCE

If the two centers line up exactly, though, gusts of wind and changes in speed and angle of attack would soon put it out of balance again. So real planes usually have the center of gravity slightly ahead of the center of lift. That makes the plane want to dive, so the tailplane (horizontal stabilizer) is tilted up slightly at the back to make a stabilizing force that pushes down. The triangle of forces holds it steady through gusts and speed changes. Most paper airplanes don't have a separate tail, but turning up the back edge of the wing has the same effect.

know what?

Some planes have short, fat wings (low aspect ratio), and others have long, thin ones (high aspect ratio). Long thin wings create less drag for the same area, but are heavier because they have to be stronger. Paper airplanes wings are usually short to keep them from bending when thrown. But they fly just fine!

low aspect ratio

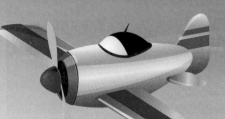

high aspect ratio

...and Stability

Planes have to be stable in more ways than just the balance of the wing. Remember, there's no one flying the plane once it leaves your hand. No little pilot, and no remote controls. So it has to be able to correct rolls, dives, and turns on its own. It needs to be stable!

A fin or vertical stabilizer is needed to keep the plane going straight. It doesn't have to be a rudder. It could be turned-up wingtips, or a big section of fuselage at the back of the plane. But it does need to be big enough to act like a weather vane and keep the plane's nose pointed straight ahead. Too little fin, and the plane will spin and crash.

The upturn of the wings is called dihedral. It helps keep the plane level. Lift pulls at right angles to each wing. It's like the plane is hanging from two strings tied together. When the plane banks, the lift created by the level wing is greater than that of the banked wing. This straightens the whole plane until the lift is equal again. With origami planes, you have to angle the wings enough that there is dihedral even after you let go and the plane relaxes!

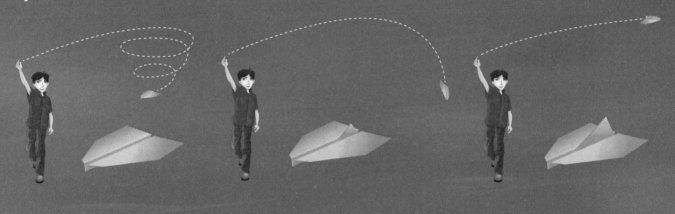

Here's a simple experiment you can try. You need a chopstick or straw, a piece of thick paper about the size of a postcard, and some glue and tape. First, cut the paper into five equal strips. Two are wrapped and glued around the nose for ballast. One is cut again to make a stabilizer and a rudder. Tape them in place. Overlap the last two strips and glue them together to make the wing. If you tape the wing over the point where the other parts balance, it should fly. What happens if you move the wing forward or back? Or remove the rudder? You'll soon see how to keep the plane stable.

Forces in Equilibrium

There are four main forces working on airplanes when they fly. We've already talked about lift and drag, but only hinted at the other two. Lift overcomes gravity, which is the force trying to pull the wing down to the ground. And thrust is the propulsive force that keeps the wing moving through the air; it works against drag.

Throw a paper airplane, and your arm provides the thrust. In a real airplane, the propeller pulls it, or the jet engine pushes it. As long as the plane is sleek and streamlined, there isn't so much drag that the plane can't keep going forward. But drag keeps it from going faster and faster, by getting stronger as the speed goes up.

What about gravity? It will always pull planes down, no matter how sleek or fast. Flight is always a struggle against gravity. A bigger engine to fly faster weighs more. Extra fuel to fly farther weighs more. A bigger plane to carry larger loads weighs more. What if there were no gravity? Well, the plane wouldn't fly. Why not? Because without gravity to balance the lift, the plane would just drift upwards instead of going straight, and without a center of gravity to pivot on, the controls would have no way of turning the plane. Gravity is needed for balance!

lift

drag

thrust

gravity

Several astronauts have actually taken paper airplanes into space. Mamoru Mohri threw one for a TV show from the Space Shuttle, Koichi Wakata did it again on the International Space Station, and Brian Binnie tossed one about the cabin of SpaceShipOne while it was weightless. But guess what? None of them flew. All three proved that lift and thrust are not enough for flight!

Wait a minute! What makes a paper airplane keep going? Crumple a piece of paper into a ball and throw it, and it curves right down to the ground. But a paper airplane keeps going forward in a more or less straight line, not falling and not slowing down. However far you can throw that ball, you can throw a paper airplane much farther. How come?

airflow

In fast level flight, lift and gravity are in balance, so the planes flies straight until drag slows it down.

airflow

When climbing, lift pulls back as well as up, so the plane slows down.

It's because lift works a little differently from gravity. Gravity always pulls straight down toward the center of the Earth, but lift pulls up at right angles to the flow of air. When you first throw your plane, it's heading straight ahead or maybe a little up, fast enough to meet the air head on. But then drag slows the plane down until it settles into a steady glide. The glide path is a long sloping line that meets the ground several yards or tens of yards away. The airplane looks like it's still going straight, but it's actually sliding down that sloping line, with the air hitting it from below the nose.

Because the lift vector is 90 degrees from the airflow, it leans forward a bit. That means that the lift is divided into two parts. Part of it holds the plane up against gravity, and part of it acts like thrust and pulls the plane forward. As long as the thrust balances drag, the speed will stay the same and the plane will keep gliding steadily until it hits the ground.

airflow

When driving, the lift pulls forward as well as up— the forward force is just enough to balance drag.

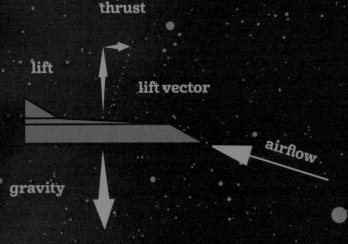

thrust

lift

lift vector

airflow

gravity

Controlling the Airplane

The Wright brothers are celebrated as the first humans to successfully fly in a heavier-than-air flying machine. But their greatest contribution, the one they patented, was their system of control. Without some way to steer in flight, airplanes would be practically useless. Here's how real planes do it.

The rudder controls the direction of flight. It can be moved left or right to push the tail in the opposite direction. When the rudder (or any other control surface) is moved, the airplane pivots around its center of gravity. This kind of motion is called yaw.

The hinged portions at the back of the horizontal stabilizers are called elevators, and as you would expect, they make the plane go up or down. Both elevators move together (though in some jets or delta planes they can move separately to function as ailerons as well). When they are turned down, they create more lift at the tail and push the nose of the plane down. When they are turned up, the tail goes down, nose goes up, and the plane climbs. This motion is called pitch.

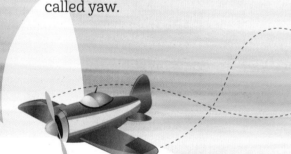

The rudder alone is not enough to make turns. Ailerons, the little hinged parts on the wingtips, are used to make the plane bank when turning. The two ailerons move in opposite directions, one up and the other down. The down aileron makes more lift on that wing, and banks it up; the up aileron pushes its wing down. Banking motions are called roll.

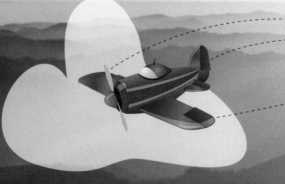

All of these surfaces can be used at the same time to create delicate and precise maneuvers. For example, ailerons and rudder can be used together to make smooth, banking turns, but unless up elevator is added, the plane sinks as it turns.

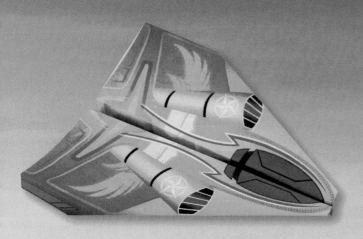

Paper airplanes often don't have separate tails or fins like real planes, so there are no ailerons or rudders to use. Instead, you have to control the plane with just the back of the wings. But that's not a big problem. Bend both sides up or down to control pitch, and one side more than the other to control roll and yaw. It's easy, once you know how it works!

On a calm day with thermal updrafts, your plane may fly a minute or more, or even go right out of sight. Thermals are big bubbles of rising warm air that form over open areas. If your plane circles inside one that rises faster than the plane sinks, it will climb with the air, like an eagle or sailplane.

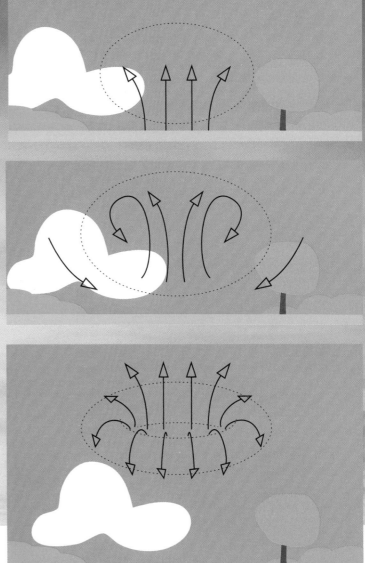

How I Got Hooked ... and You Will Too

In my family, if you wanted something, you made it yourself. There probably wasn't a lot of money to buy things, but that wasn't the point. It was more fun making our own stuff, and the clothes, furniture, and toys we made seemed better—were better—than anything that came from a store.

One of my earliest memories is of making paper airplanes. I used to wake up early, well before everyone else in my family, so I had lots of time to play by myself. I had a pile of old used paper, and I made airplane after airplane, flying them and putting the best ones in a box. I remember having invented a squid airplane on my own. Someone threw the box out one day, and I still wonder what treasures were lost when it went.

I made a lot of models, mostly from paper. I liked paper because I could find lots around the house, and it didn't require any tools fancier than scissors and glue. I made models of houses, cars, and ships, but I liked airplanes best of all. That's because flying models are not just models, but real airplanes! I borrowed all the paper airplane books in the library and made every single plane in them. The two shown above were favorites.

There was an excellent science museum near my house in Toronto, called the Ontario Science Centre, and it often had paper airplane contests. I found that with a good design and careful adjustment, I could usually win them. Unlike sports, this was something I could be good at!

THE GREAT INTERNATIONAL PAPER AIRPLANE BOOK

By JERRY MANDER GEORGE DIPPEL AND HOWARD GOSSAGE

THE OFFICIAL FLY-THEM-YO PLANES—WITH TECHNICAL DA ALOFT RECORDS, PHOTOGRAPHS AND THE FIRST INTERNATIONAL PAPER AIRPLA CONDUCTED BY SCIENTIFIC AMERICAN

HOW TO MAKE & FLY PAPER AIRPLANES
by Captain Ralph S. Barnaby, U.S. Navy (Ret.)

In the summer of 1974, the Ontario Science Centre hosted a handicraft exposition called "In Praise of Hands." There was a hand-made toy booth, and for one week I sat in it and taught passersby how to make great paper airplanes. All those contests had paid off!

Paper airplanes are all about experimenting and having fun. You don't know if a design will fly until you try it! But because you're using paper, you can easily make all kinds of shapes in a few minutes or hours, and try them out right away. If your new design doesn't fly, just get out a new sheet of paper and try to improve it. And when it flies great, you'll feel great! What could be more fun than that?

Here are two books that changed my life. I found Jet-Age Jamboree, by Yasuaki Ninomiya, at the library. I was so excited that I borrowed scissors and glue from the librarian and made one of the planes right there. The more I made, the more excited I was. I sent the author a letter and some of my own designs, and he sent me one of his Japanese books. I couldn't read Japanese, but I got a dictionary and tried. This set me on the path to Japan!

All Kinds of Paper Airplanes

When you think about paper airplanes, it's probably origami airplanes that you think of first. When you talk about paper airplanes with your friends, they're probably imagining paper darts. But there are many other kinds of paper airplane. So many kinds, in fact, that they hardly have anything in common. Except, of course, that they fly, and that they're made of paper. You'll see a gallery of photographs of some of them on the following pages.

The great thing about origami is that you can make an airplane in a minute or two with nothing but a piece of paper and your fingers. Above right is the Orbit from my *Simple Origami Airplanes* mini kit. It's made with just a 5-inch square of paper, and can fly for more than 12 seconds.

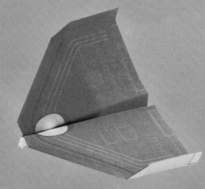

Add a tiny bit of tape, and the possibilities really explode. Below is the Space Shuttle from my *Simple Origami Airplanes* kit.

Cut-and-Paste Planes

If you use scissors to cut the paper a little, the possibilities expand again. You can cut the wings and tail into interesting shapes, like the Mt. Fuji plane below, designed by Kazumichi Mochizuki. The parts are folded and stapled together.

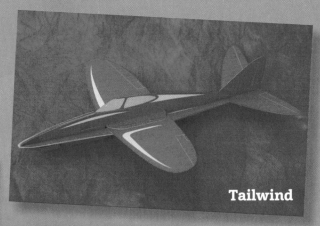

Tailwind

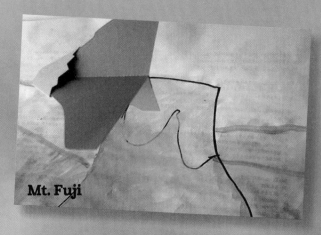

Mt. Fuji

The plane below is made from a postcard (with a design printed on it). In this case, the paper is glued together. It's very, very simple, but it will fly a long, long way!

The more like an airplane they become, the better they will fly. Below is the Osprey, from an upcoming kit, and at top right is a shot of the Tailwind, from my *One Minute Paper Airplanes* kit. They are just thick paper, cut and stapled together, but they can be flown outdoors, and go quite a long way!

Postcard

Osprey

Realistic Planes

With a little more time and effort, you can make airplanes that really look like airplanes, and fly just like them too!

Yasuaki Ninomiya of Japan pioneered the style of profile model airplanes, with fuselages made of layers of paper glued together. They are launched with a rubber band catapult, and can fly for a minute or more. Below left is a competition plane designed in the Ninomiya style.

Instead of laminated fuselages, I tried making even more realistic 3-D ones. I had a lot of failures at first, but after a while my planes got better—better looking, and better flying. Below middle and right are two examples, both of which fly great! In the middle is the Sidewinder, which is designed to fly high and long. It's in my *High Performance Paper Airplanes* kit, along with the scale Grumman Corsair on the right. It looks like a real plane in flight!

Ninomiya style

Sidewinder

Grumman Corsair

Go Wild!

Almost anything is possible! As long as you have wings and balance, all kinds of strange paper airplanes are possible. The only thing holding you back now is your imagination!

Below is a jumbo paper airplane, made of cardboard and tissue paper. The wings are 2.5 meters (almost 8 feet) across! It was designed and built by a team of engineering students led by Takumi Tomita, and flew clear across the gymnasium. And I've seen people fly even bigger jumbo planes—some the size of a real Cessna!

A flying Christmas tree, a flying crocodile, a flying fish ... if you can think of it, you can build and fly it!

Jumbo airplane

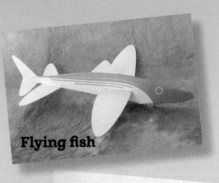

Flying fish

Flying crocodile

Flying Christmas tree

Folding Techniques

All of these planes are easy to fold, once you know how to read the instructions. I've drawn them with some symbols that are standard in all origami books, plus one or two of my own.

There are only two ways to fold paper: mountain folds and valley folds. For valley folds, you fold the paper towards you. For mountain folds, you fold it away. Most of the folds in this book are valley folds.

This is a valley fold; it looks a bit like a valley.

And this is a mountain fold.

To make it really easy, the origami paper in this book already has the folding lines printed on the front and back, so every fold is a valley fold! Just follow the numbers.

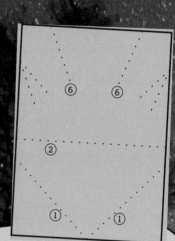

What the Arrows Mean

Fold this way

Fold around behind

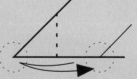

The centers of circles show which points to bring together when folding.

Fold and reopen

Flip the whole plane over

Bracket marks indicate things of the same width, such as the resulting flaps when you fold halfway along an edge.

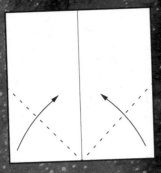

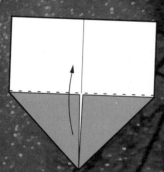

Most planes start with the paper face down. The drawings show the front of the paper in dark colors, and the back in lighter colors.

Folding is a lot easier if you fold the loose edges away from you. Line up the edges or corners carefully, double check, and then crease the paper.

The best way to crease is to start from the middle, and run your finger first to the left, then to the right. Hold the paper tightly so the corners don't move!

Finally, burnish the fold to make it really sharp. You can run your thumbnail along the crease, or use a tool like a pen cap.

Most of the planes need a final tweak to really fly well. They will dive until you bend up the back edge of the wing slightly. Bending the wing keeps the nose up and lets the plane float on the air. But bend too much, and it will stall and crash. Add and subtract until the plane flies just right.

Fold away from you

Crease from the middle

Burnish the fold

Bend the wings

A Word About Paper

What's the best kind of paper for paper airplanes? Well, almost any paper will do, but you especially want something light and stiff, which holds a crease. Newspaper is too floppy. The glossy paper used for ads and magazines won't hold a crease: as soon as you let go, the airplane starts unfolding itself! The special origami paper called kami is best, but it's hard to find and usually only comes in squares. That leaves ordinary white copy paper. It's a bit thick, but it's stiff, holds a crease, and comes in rectangles. And you can get it anywhere! Not perfect, but close!

Here's a little secret about the planes in this book. They're made with paper that's an unusual shape, a little slimmer than letter, but fatter than A4. That means you can fold the planes with either size of paper, and they'll still fly great! If you want to make the paper the same size as in this book, here's how. But remember: it's a secret!

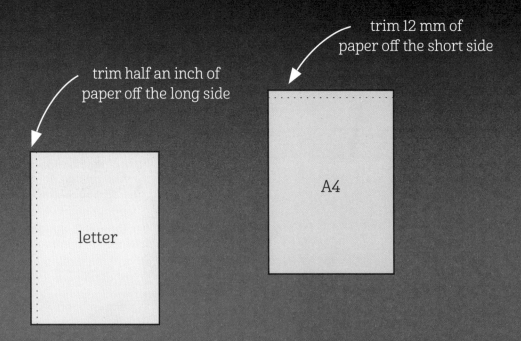

trim half an inch of
paper off the long side

trim 12 mm of
paper off the short side

letter

A4

Scissors & Tape—Optional!

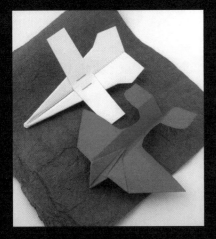

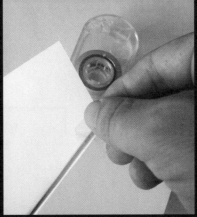

CUTTING

Is it okay to cut the paper? Origami people usually say no. Origami airplanes usually use one piece of uncut paper. If you can make a great plane just by folding the paper, that's great. But if you're playing on your own, what's wrong with a little cutting? See what happens. Your plane will be great!

TAPING

How about tape, glue, and staples? Most people say no. But you can use tape for Guinness World Record airplanes, so I think that means yes! Glue and staples are against the "rules," but that doesn't mean you can't use them on planes you make just for yourself!

WOW!

If you do use tape, just a little bit to hold the wings or tail in place is enough. You can see the difference a tiny piece can make! When you tape the plane together like this, it will fly a lot faster and farther, but the balance will be different, so you might have to turn up the back of the wings a lot to keep it from crashing.

Test Flying

Your plane won't fly well unless it's straight. Hold it at arm's length and check.

If it's not, carefully twist the wings and tail until everything is straight and flat.

Test fly the plane by tossing it firmly straight forward and watching how it flies. If it stalls, dives or turns, adjust it as shown on the facing page and test fly it again, until it glides gently.

Remember, paper airplanes are made from paper, so they bend in crash landings, or in damp weather. You will have to tweak them again from time to time. If they stop flying well, check that they are straight, test fly them again, and they'll go back to being great!

If your plane is out of alignment, make minor adjustments to take your plane from this...

...to this

Straighten the wings and tail

The plane should be straight

Test the plane

28

If your planes stalls or dives, adjust it until it glides straight, as in pattern A.

A

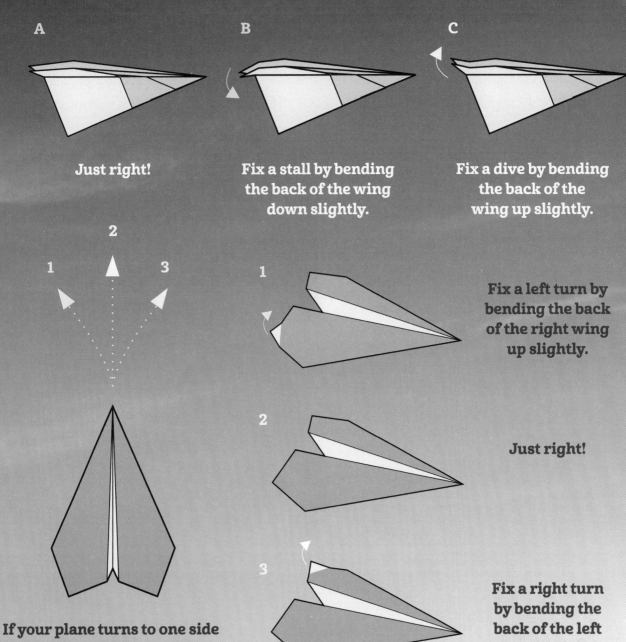

Just right!

B

Fix a stall by bending the back of the wing down slightly.

C

Fix a dive by bending the back of the wing up slightly.

1

Fix a left turn by bending the back of the right wing up slightly.

2

Just right!

3

Fix a right turn by bending the back of the left wing up slightly.

If your plane turns to one side or the other, adjust it until it flies straight as in pattern 2.

29

Higher and Farther

Every plane has its own way of flying. Some are fast, and some are slow. Some need a good throw, and some you toss gently. Which is which? Here's a hint: be gentle with wide wings, but throw pointy planes hard!

The Flying Wing (page 40) has no fuselage to hang onto when you throw it, so you have to pinch it between your finger and thumb, as demonstrated below, and push it forward. Did it sort of dive to the floor? You didn't push hard enough. Did it pop up to the ceiling and crash? Whoa, way to hard! When you get it just right, the plane will swoop right across the room.

Most of the other planes in this book have a fuselage to hold onto. Pinch it between your finger and thumb right where it balances (as in the bottom photo), and give it a good toss. If there is enough room, you can throw a little harder, but still basically straight ahead. Be sure not to hit anyone, break anything, or poke any eyes!

Without fuselage

With fuselage

On calm, dry days you can take your planes out to the park. After a few test flights, try throwing them as hard and high as you can. How long can you make yours fly?

Try throwing the plane straight ahead at first. If you aim too high, the plane will probably stall and fall. You want it to go into a glide. One trick is to bank the airplane away from you when you throw it. That way, it will turn in a big circle and get good air before the speed runs out.

Banking the plane as you release it will allow it to spiral for a longer flight.

Test flight

Then again, planes like the Fireball (page 42), the Chevron (page 44) and the Delta Jet (page 48) are designed to go almost straight up. If you want a really long flight, you need to get your plane as high as possible. The higher it goes, the longer it takes to glide back down to the ground!

This is how world record holders launch their planes. Start with the plane down near the ground, and use your legs and back as well as you arms. Don't snap the plane, though, because it will just twirl and flutter. A long, smooth throw with a follow-through keeps the plane going straight. You'll be amazed at how high it can go.

The Ring Wraith (page 50) is different from the other planes, because it spins as it flies. It's a little tricky to throw at first, but with a bit of practice it will go amazing distances. Grip it lightly with your right hand, as shown to the right. Set it spinning with a downward flick of your fingers as you throw it forward. It's a lot like throwing a football. The faster it spins, the farther it will go.

Are your planes flying right? Then take them out to the park, or to a really big gym, and see how far they'll go! You'll probably attract an audience. Give them the show of their lives!

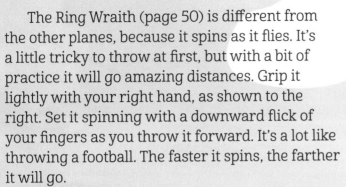

Belly Button

A plane with a belly button? Well, this plane has one! We learned to make dart planes in school, but in Japan, kids learn one sort of like this. That little triangle holding it all together (see step 6)? That's the belly button.

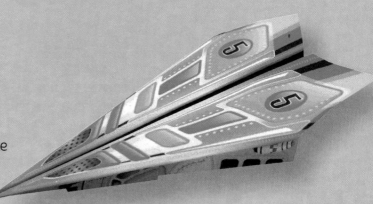

1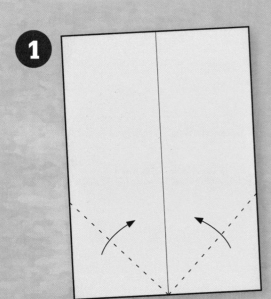

Start with the paper face down. Fold the two bottom corners in to the center on the 1 lines.

2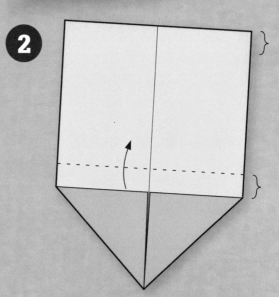

Fold the bottom part of the paper up on line 2. The next step shows how the extra width at the top and bottom will be about the same.

3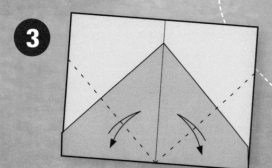

Fold and unfold the new bottom corners on the 3 lines.

4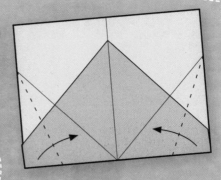

Fold the corners on the 4 lines, so the edges touch the creases you made in the last step.

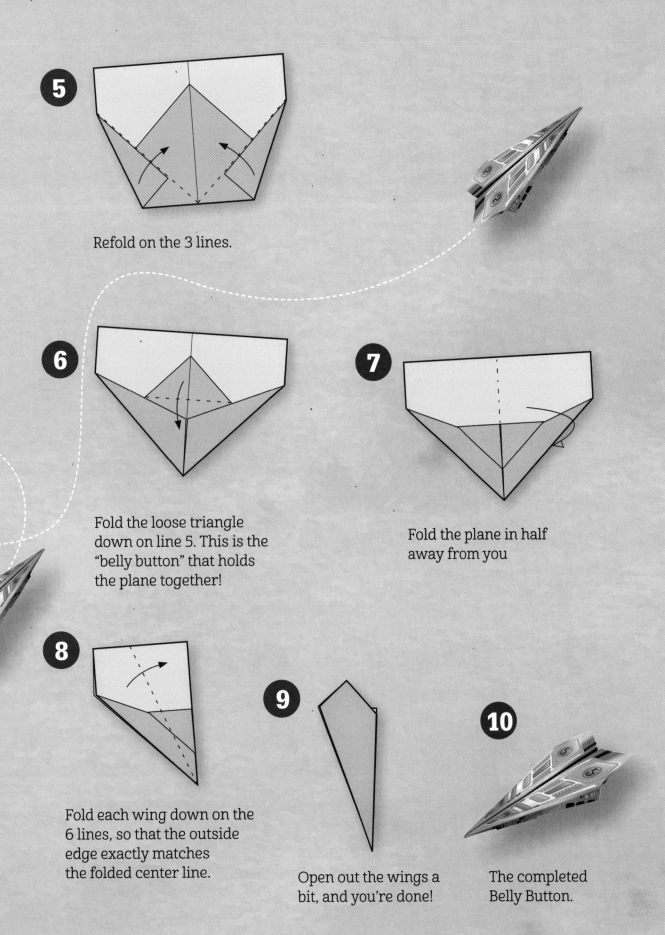

5

Refold on the 3 lines.

6

Fold the loose triangle down on line 5. This is the "belly button" that holds the plane together!

7

Fold the plane in half away from you

8

Fold each wing down on the 6 lines, so that the outside edge exactly matches the folded center line.

9

Open out the wings a bit, and you're done!

10

The completed Belly Button.

Decapod

Did you know squid can fly?
This one sure can! It looks bizarre, but
it flies great. Right across the room!
Right down the hall! Right out of sight!

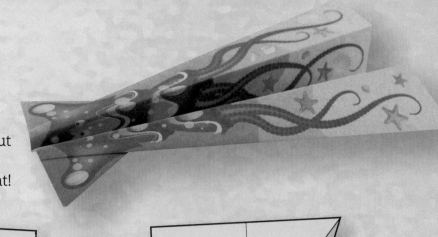

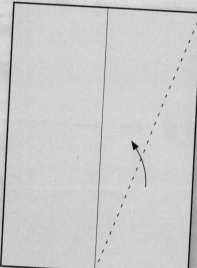

Start with the paper facing
down. Fold one corner
along one line 1 from the
center to the top corner.

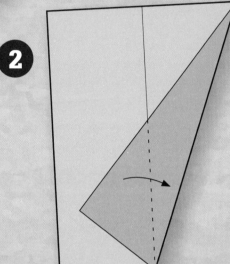

Fold that corner back along
the center line on line 2.

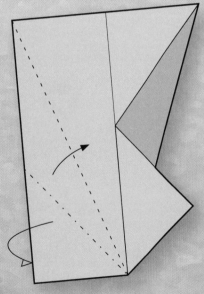

Repeat the first two steps
for the other corner.

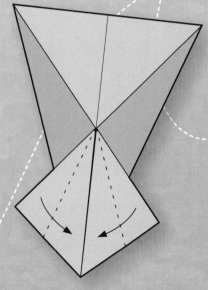

Fold the two corners in to the
center line along the 3 lines.

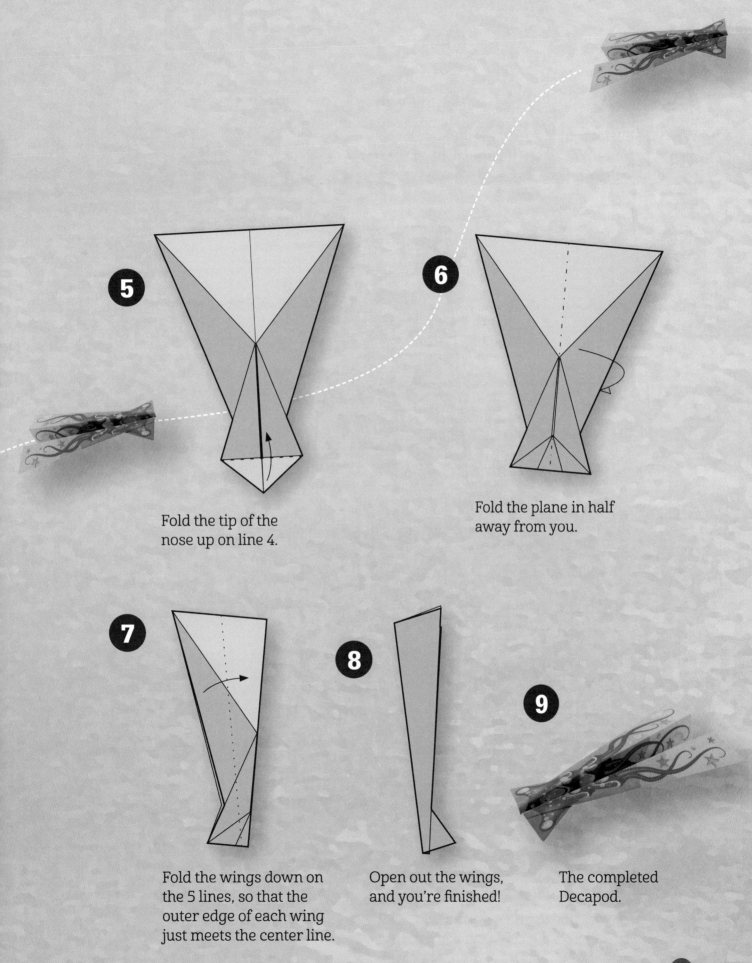

5 Fold the tip of the nose up on line 4.

6 Fold the plane in half away from you.

7 Fold the wings down on the 5 lines, so that the outer edge of each wing just meets the center line.

8 Open out the wings, and you're finished!

9 The completed Decapod.

Hammerhead

What if sharks could fly? That would make a great horror movie. Here's a hammerhead shark to get the story going.

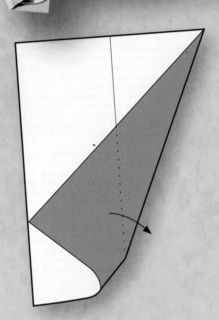

1

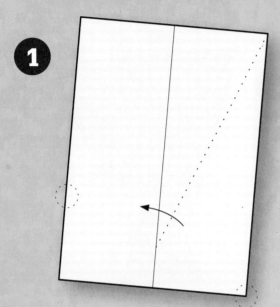

Start with the paper face down. Fold the bottom right corner across to the opposite edge. Crease on line 1 as far as the center line.

2

Fold the corner back outwards on line 2.

3

Repeat the first two steps on the other side, with lines 3 and 4. You should have a kind of pocket at the bottom.

4

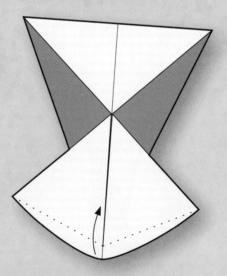

Crease the pocket flat along the 5 lines.

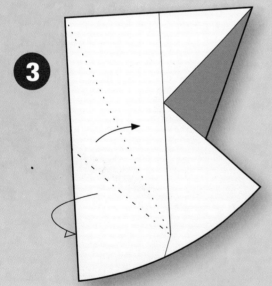

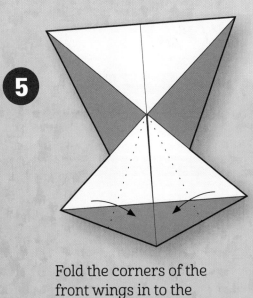

5 Fold the corners of the front wings in to the center on the 6 lines.

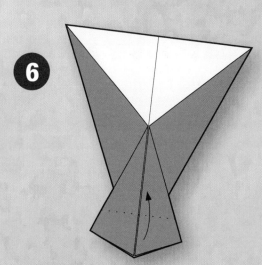

6 Fold the front up on line 7. This is where the edge of the paper underneath is.

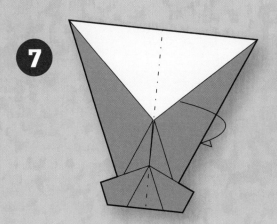

7 Fold the plane in half away from you.

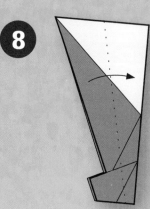

8 Fold the wings down on the 8 lines, so that the outer edges just meet the center line.

9 Open out the wings, and you're done!

10

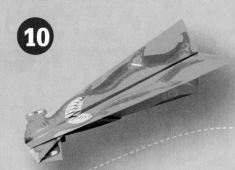

The completed Hammerhead.

Flying Wing

The simplest kind of plane is one that's just a wing. It whizzes, it swoops, and it flies really fast! And it's stealthy too. No one will ever catch this plane on their radar!

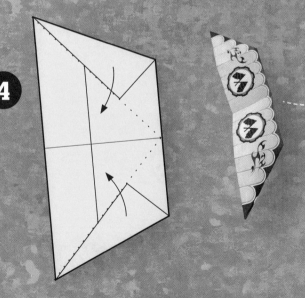

1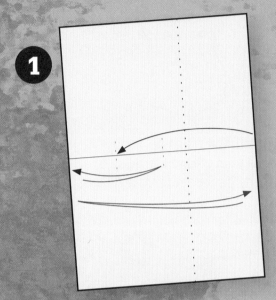

Start with the paper face down. Fold along line 1. The red arrows show how to find the spot on a plain piece of paper.

2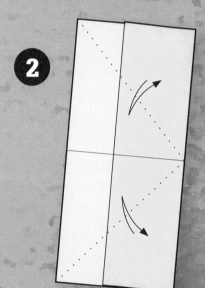

Fold and unfold the front corners along the 2 lines, from the back corners to the center line.

3

Fold the front corners in to the creases from the last step, along the 3 lines.

4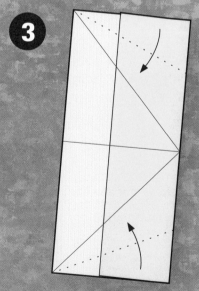

Refold the corners on the 2 lines.

5

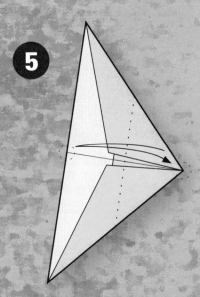

Fold the front half back on line 4 to the center of the rear edge, and unfold it.

6

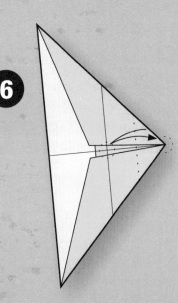

Now, fold the front quarter back on line 5 to the center of the crease you just made, and unfold it.

7

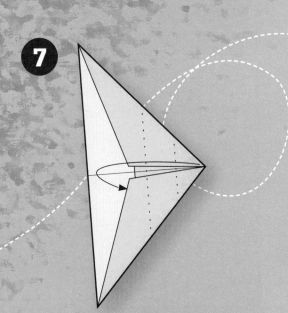

Refold on lines 4 and 5, and tuck the tip under the two flaps.

8

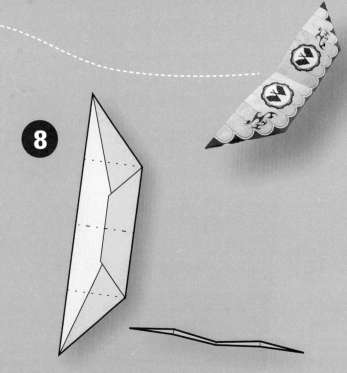

Valley fold the wingtips slightly on the 6 lines, and mountain fold the center line just a little, so that it looks like the small picture above when seen from the front. All done!

Fireball

Here's a plane you can throw really hard. It's good and heavy at the front, so it will go fast and straight, like a rocket plane!

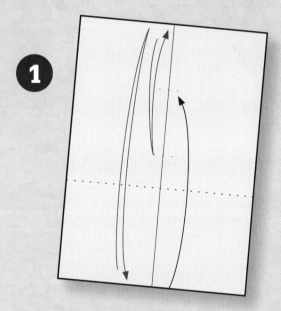

1 Start with the paper face down. Fold along line 1. The red arrows show how to find the spot on a plain piece of paper.

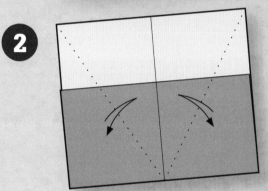

2 Fold and unfold the front corners along the 2 lines, from the back corners to the center line.

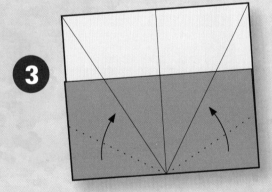

3 Fold the front corners in to the creases from the last step, along the 3 lines.

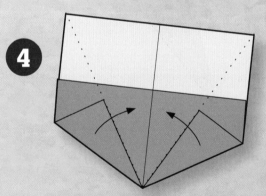

4 Refold the corners on the 2 lines.

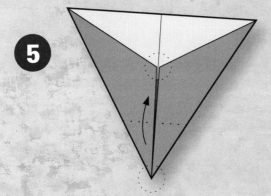

5 Fold the tip of the nose up on line 4 to the place shown.

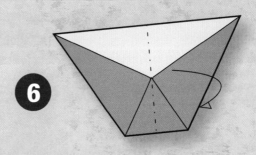

6 Fold the plane in half away from you.

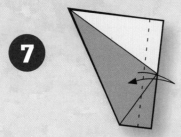

7 Fold and unfold the wings on the 5 lines.

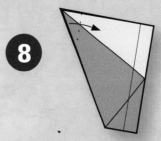

8 Fold down the wingtips on the 6 lines.

9 Open the wings out. If the plane looks like this from the front, you're ready to fly!

Chevron

The only thing holding this plane back is your arm! How fast can you throw? 'Cause this plane is fast!

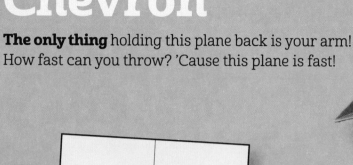

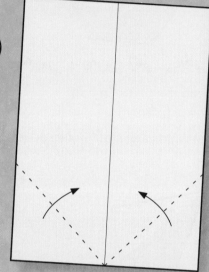

1

Start with the paper face down. Fold the two bottom corners in to the center on the 1 lines.

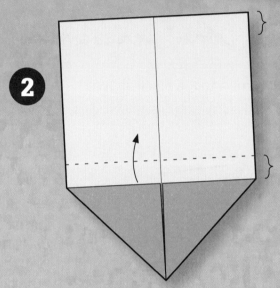

2

Fold the bottom part of the paper up on line 2. The next step shows how the extra width at the top and bottom will be about the same.

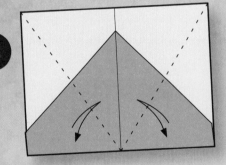

3

Fold and unfold the new bottom corners on the 3 lines.

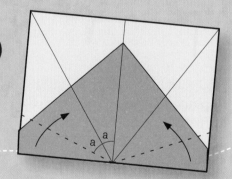

4

Fold the corners on the 4 lines. The "a" angles should be equal. Look at step 6 to see why.

5

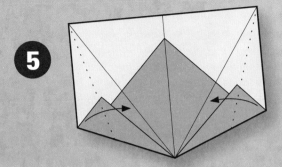

Fold the corners again on the 5 lines.

6

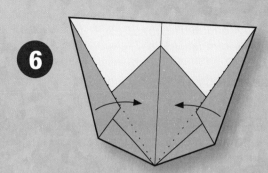

Refold the corners on the 3 lines.

7

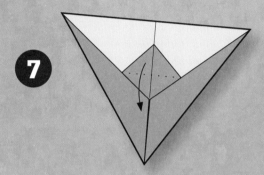

The edges will just meet in the center! Now fold the belly button down on line 6.

8

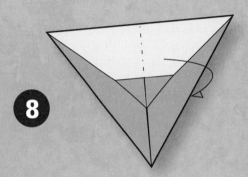

Fold the plane in half away from you.

9

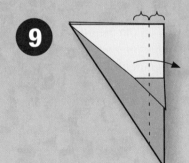

Fold the wings down on the 7 lines. The fold is half the width of the belly button and parallel to the center line.

10

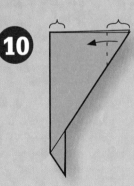

Fold up the rudders on the 8 lines. The height of the rudder is one and a half times the width of the fold you made in step 9.

11

Open out the wings and rudders so that they look like this from the front. All done!

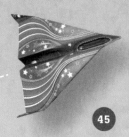

Spade

Slow and steady. Check out the way the Spade floats! It uses Takuo Toda's amazing nose lock mechanism to hold the plane together. This one will go right across the room with just a light toss. Dig that Spade!

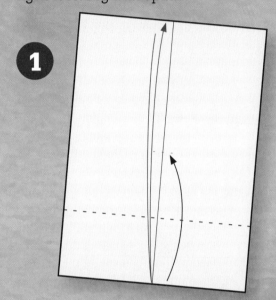

1

Start with the paper face down. Fold the bottom quarter up on line 1. The red arrow shows how to find the spot on a plain piece of paper.

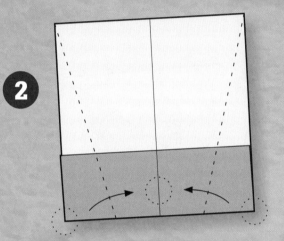

2

Fold the two front corners on the 2 lines, so they just touch the center line as shown.

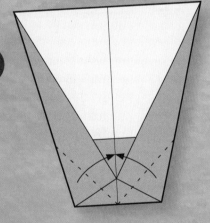

3

Fold the new corners on the 3 lines, so they meet at the center line as shown.

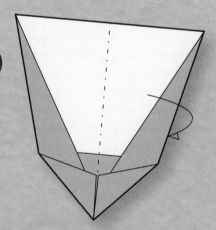

4

Fold the plane in half away from you.

5

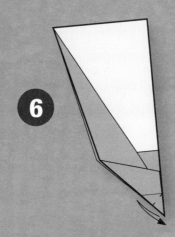

Fold the nose up on line 4 to the point shown, and unfold it.

6

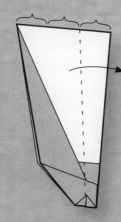

Fold the tip up on line 5 to the end of crease 4, and unfold it.

7

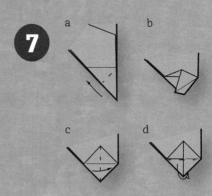

a and b: Squash fold the nose as shown. c: Fold the top layer down on line 6. d: Fold the tip around to the other side.

The nose fold, seen from below.

8

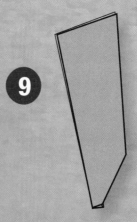

Fold the wings down on the 7 lines. They start at the middle of the nose, and end one third of the way across the back edge.

9

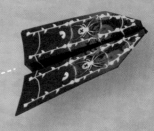

Straighten out the wings, and you're ready to fly!

10

The completed Spade.

Delta Jet

Want to win a distance contest? This may be the plane to do it. You can throw it really hard, thanks the nose lock fold. Throw it high! It will go straight and far. Try it in the gym, but the wall's the limit!

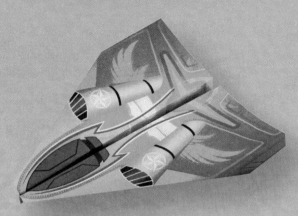

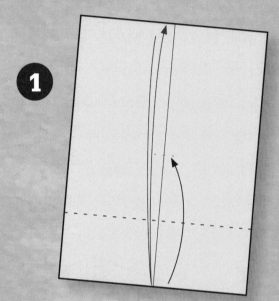

1

Start with the paper face down. Fold the bottom quarter up on line 1. The red arrow shows how to find the spot on a plain piece of paper.

2

Fold on the 2 lines so the two corners meet at the center of the flap you folded in step one.

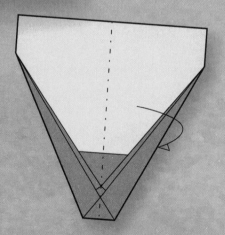

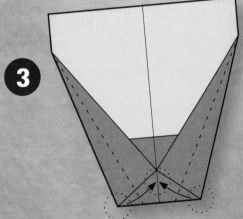

3

Fold the new corners in on the 3 lines, starting at the same places as the last folds and meeting at the center line.

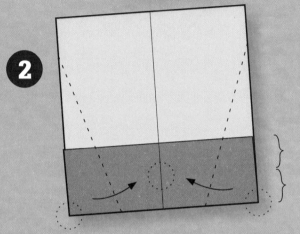

4

Fold the plane in half away from you.

5

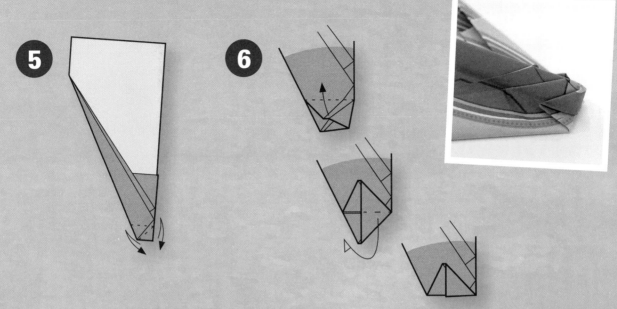

Fold and unfold on lines 4 and 5. Line 4 starts where the wing edge gets thick, and line 5 makes the front edge meet the new crease.

6

Lock the nose by pulling the top corner up and back over the fuselage, and folding the lower corner back around the other side of the nose.

7

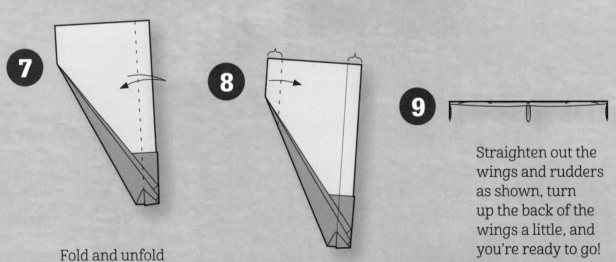

Fold and unfold the wings on the 6 lines. Fold them down as far as you can at the front, with the crease running parallel to the center line.

8

Fold down the wingtip rudder on line 7. The width of the rudder is the same as the width of the fuselage. Do the same for the other wingtip.

9

Straighten out the wings and rudders as shown, turn up the back of the wings a little, and you're ready to go!

Ring Wraith

You throw it like a football, and it flies like a flying disk. It zooms and speeds up. Is it really a plane? What kind of magic is it?

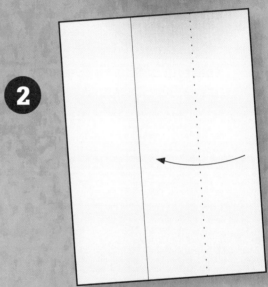

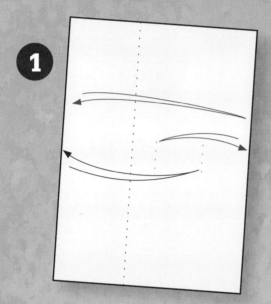

1

Start with the paper face down. Fold and unfold line 1. The red arrows show how to find the spot on a plain piece of paper.

2

Fold the right edge to the crease on line 2.

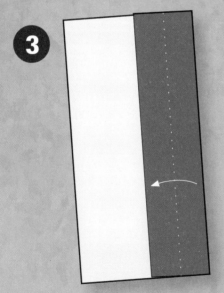

3

Fold the new right edge to the crease on line 3.

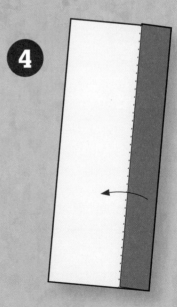

4

Refold line 1.

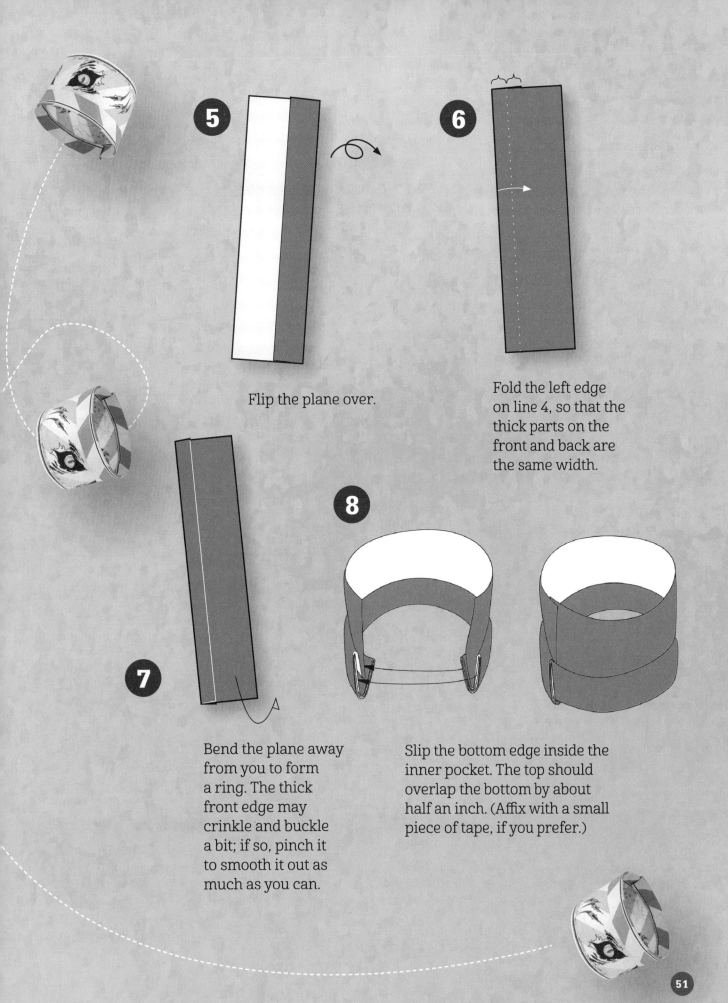

5 Flip the plane over.

6 Fold the left edge on line 4, so that the thick parts on the front and back are the same width.

7 Bend the plane away from you to form a ring. The thick front edge may crinkle and buckle a bit; if so, pinch it to smooth it out as much as you can.

8 Slip the bottom edge inside the inner pocket. The top should overlap the bottom by about half an inch. (Affix with a small piece of tape, if you prefer.)

Space Cruiser

This plane has a couple of tricky folds, so look at all the steps before you try it. But then get ready to blast off for a galaxy far, far away!

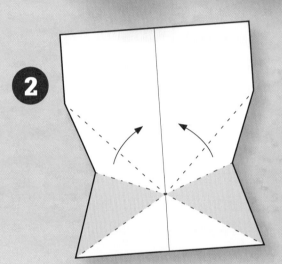

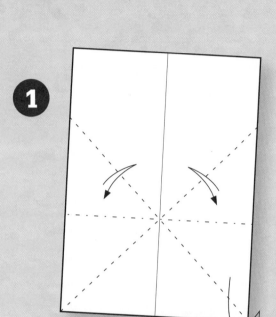

Start with the paper face down. Valley fold and unfold lines 1 and 2. Mountain fold and unfold line 3.

Pull the paper up at the ends of line 3 so the corners met at the center line. Step 3 shows how the finished fold will look.

Fold the two loose corners down to the front tip on the 4 lines.

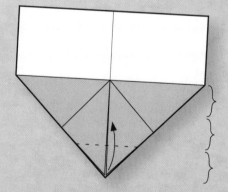

Fold the whole tip up on line 5. The diagram shows how to find the place to fold.

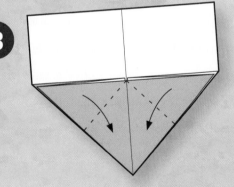

5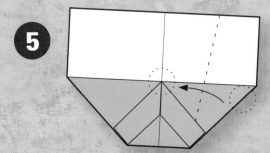

Fold one side of the plane on line 6, starting at the front corner and slipping the side under the front layers as far as it will go.

6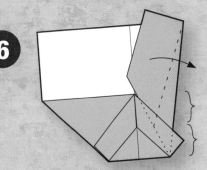

Fold the paper back out on line 7. The fold starts halfway along the hidden part of the edge.

7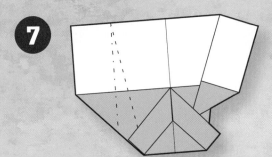

Fold the other side the same way.

8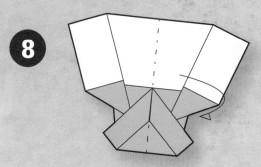

Fold the plane in half away from you.

9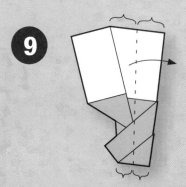

Fold the wings down on the 8 lines. The fold starts and ends at halfway points.

10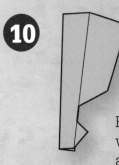

Fold out the wings a bit and you're ready for launch!

Raptor

With just the right wing adjustment, this powerful model will circle as if searching for prey.

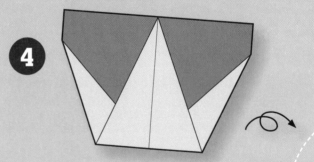

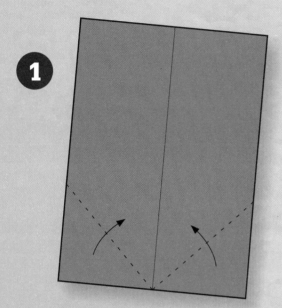

1

Start with the paper face down. Fold the front corners to the center line on the 1 lines.

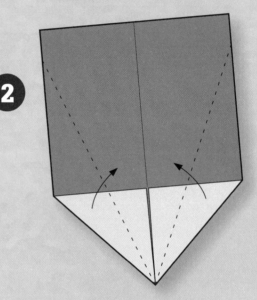

2

Fold the new corners to the center line on the 2 lines.

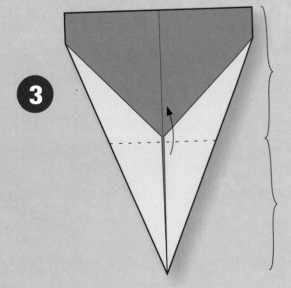

3

Fold the tip up to the back edge of the paper on line 3.

4

Flip the plane over.

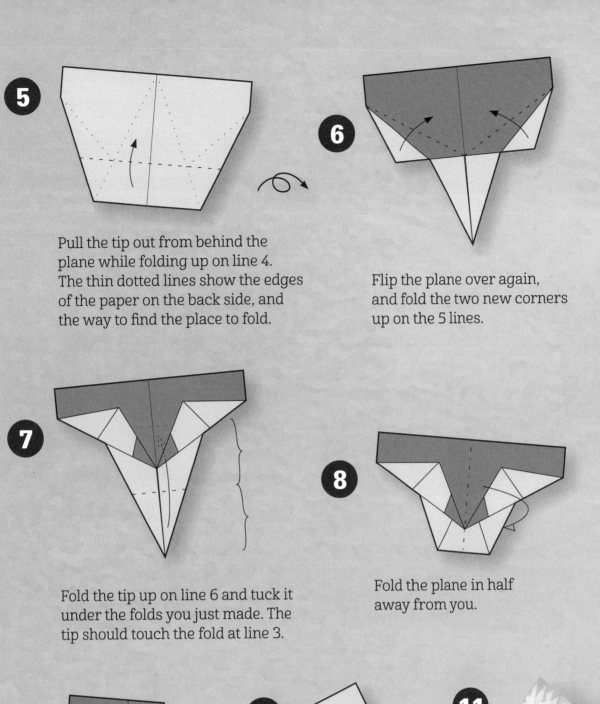

5 Pull the tip out from behind the plane while folding up on line 4. The thin dotted lines show the edges of the paper on the back side, and the way to find the place to fold.

6 Flip the plane over again, and fold the two new corners up on the 5 lines.

7 Fold the tip up on line 6 and tuck it under the folds you just made. The tip should touch the fold at line 3.

8 Fold the plane in half away from you.

9 Fold the wings down on the 7 lines. The side of the nose should meet the center line.

10 Open the wings out, and you're ready to go!

11 The completed Raptor.

Iceberg

Both wings don't have to be the same shape for the plane to be amazing! No one will believe it will fly—until you show them. Incredibly cool!

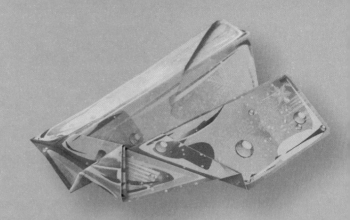

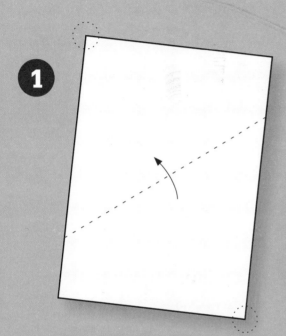

1 Start with the paper face up. Fold the bottom right corner to the top left corner on line 1.

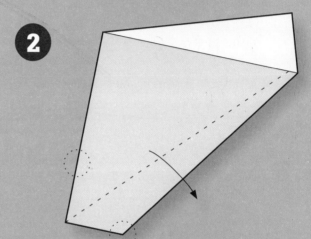

2 Fold the top corner down on line 2. The left edge should just match the bottom edge.

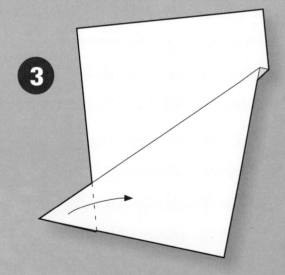

3 Fold the triangular bit on line 3 as shown.

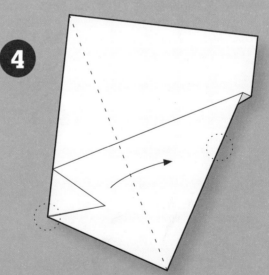

4 Fold the paper on line 4 as shown. The bottom edge should just meet the right edge.

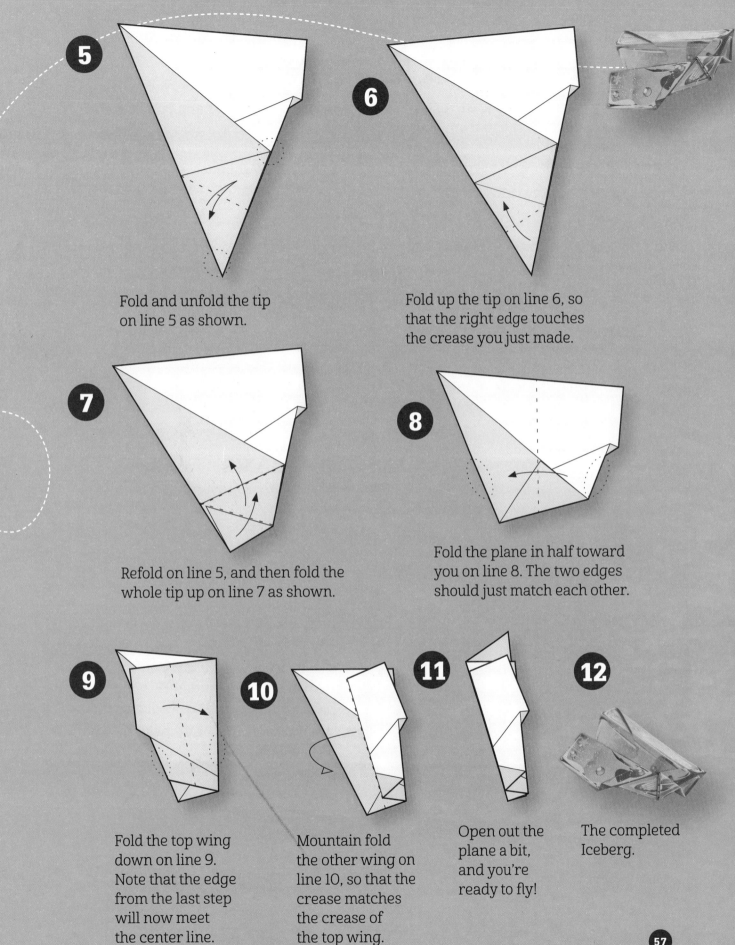

5

Fold and unfold the tip on line 5 as shown.

6

Fold up the tip on line 6, so that the right edge touches the crease you just made.

7

Refold on line 5, and then fold the whole tip up on line 7 as shown.

8

Fold the plane in half toward you on line 8. The two edges should just match each other.

9

Fold the top wing down on line 9. Note that the edge from the last step will now meet the center line.

10

Mountain fold the other wing on line 10, so that the crease matches the crease of the top wing.

11

Open out the plane a bit, and you're ready to fly!

12

The completed Iceberg.

Games and Contests

Once your planes are all folded up, you're going to be having fun flying them. But just tossing them around a room might start to get dull after a while. Why not get together with friends to play paper airplane games, or try competing to see who is the best paper airplane pilot? Here are some great games and contest hints.

SAFETY

Before we start throwing planes, let's think about safety. I can't say enough about it. Keep in mind that your planes are pointy and thrown at high speed, and you'll likely be flying with other people around.

Make sure you stay far enough away from others that your plane won't hit them. This is especially important in a contest, where everyone will be pushing the limits of the planes. Never throw your planes at people or animals. Stay away from busy streets and power lines, and don't go after planes that have landed in dangerous places. It isn't worth it! You can always just fold up another one!

RING TOSS GAME

This game isn't exactly a ring toss (unless you're using the Ring Wraith!), but it's the same sort of idea. Set up a number of open boxes of different sizes or at different distances. Smaller or farther boxes earn more points. Players stand behind a line and try to fly their planes into the boxes. Planes that go in get points, and the most points win. Turn the boxes so the open side is facing up if you want to make it even harder. Do you have some hula hoops? You could set those up too. Flaming rings? Just kidding— no flaming rings!

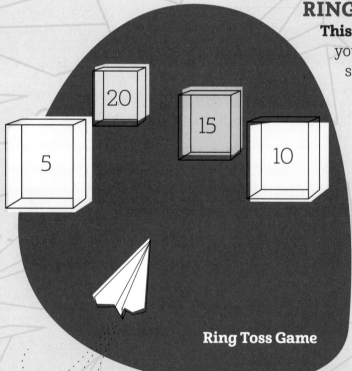

Ring Toss Game

STEEPLECHASE GAME

Take those hula hoops, or pieces of cardboard with holes cut in them, and set them up in a course around your lawn—or in a gym, if you have one. The idea is to fly your planes from a starting line through each of the holes in turn, beginning each new flight where the last one ended. How fast can you go around the course? How about if you and your friends are racing?

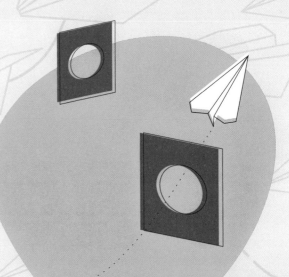

Steeplechase Game

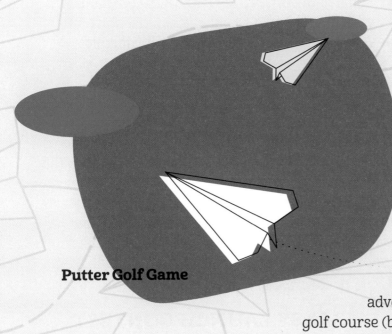

Putter Golf Game

PUTTER GOLF GAME

Put a number of targets on the floor or grass, and try to land your plane on them. Keep flying the plane until it lands on the mark, and add one stroke for each flight. The person who goes around the course with the lowest score wins! If you're really adventurous, you could try this on a real golf course (but only with permission!).

CURLING GAME

To curl, you need a slippery wood floor, like a gym floor. Mark some bulls-eye circles on the floor with tape. Players form two teams, and take turns throwing their planes from behind a line (about 5 to 10 yards from the mark), trying to land in the middle of the bulls-eye. If there's a rival plane there already, knock it out of the way! You can either play for points, or let the plane closest to the center be the outright winner.

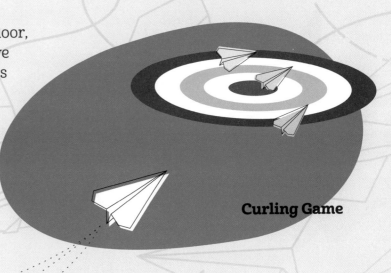

Curling Game

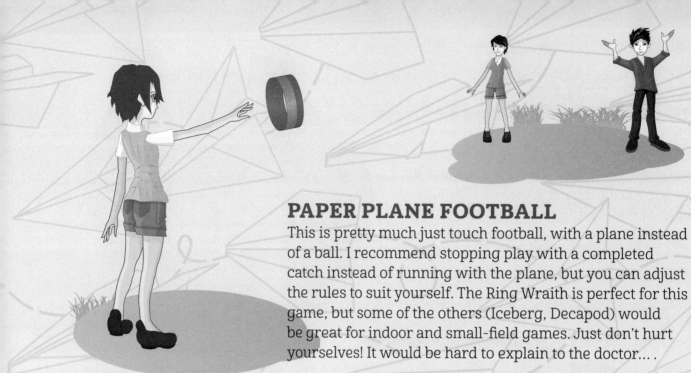

PAPER PLANE FOOTBALL

This is pretty much just touch football, with a plane instead of a ball. I recommend stopping play with a completed catch instead of running with the plane, but you can adjust the rules to suit yourself. The Ring Wraith is perfect for this game, but some of the others (Iceberg, Decapod) would be great for indoor and small-field games. Just don't hurt yourselves! It would be hard to explain to the doctor... .

TIME AND DISTANCE CONTESTS

Most paper airplane contests measure time or distance. You could try acrobatics too, but they are very hard to judge. Distance is judged by measuring in a straight line from the launch site to where the plane first touches the ground or a wall. The trick is in getting the plane to fly straight! Distance contests are fun in gymnasiums, but outside they get very difficult very quickly, as pilots become proficient. Once you go past the end of a fifty-yard tape measure, the judging becomes a chore. Using a stopwatch to time is much easier. Start the watch the moment the plane is launched, and stop it when the plane touches the ground, hits an obstacle and stops, or disappears from sight. Take the total time from several flights to choose a winner.

MASS LAUNCH CONTEST

Here is a simple idea to help reduce the role of luck in the contest. It's the mass launch, where everyone launches their plane at the same time and place, and the last one to touch the ground wins. This works well because everyone shares the same wind and space, but it might be hard for judges to watch a large bunch of planes at once. This makes a great tie-in to a workshop or a school class; all the participants build the same model, and compete over trimming and flying skills.

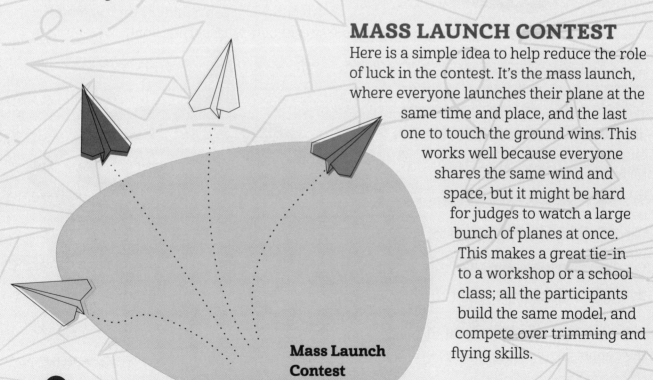

Mass Launch Contest

Organizing a Contest

Don't try too much at once. Do your first contest as a pick-up with friends, or part of a school or scout or 4-H event. Don't aim for a bigger group until you have some experience. Try a number of different ideas to see what works best for you and your friends. You need to think about these things:

A place like a gym, a park, or a schoolyard, and permission to use it.

A date, a time, and an announcement.

Rules.

Safety.

Judges and timers.

Weather, if you'll be outside, and a plan for what to do if it rains.

Something for the winners: prizes or bragging rights.

Event insurance, just in case.

To make it a little easier, here are a couple of score sheets you can start with. They both have two classes. One is used for time or distance, and the other for a contest using either a standard plane (in this case Delta Jet) or any other plane the pilot wishes. But of course, feel free to change them to match your own rules.

Toronto Paper Pilots Contest
Pilot's name _____
Class: ☐ Time ☐ Distance
Score:
1 _____ seconds/feet
2 _____ seconds/feet
3 _____ seconds/feet
4 _____ seconds/feet
5 _____ seconds/feet
Total _____ seconds/feet

Flying Colors Contest
Pilot's name _____
Class: ☐ Free ☐ Delta Jet
Score:
1 _____ seconds/feet
2 _____ seconds/feet
3 _____ seconds/feet
4 _____ seconds/feet
5 _____ seconds/feet
Total _____ seconds/feet

One hundred-fifty people took part in this origami airplane contest in Miyakojima, Okinawa. Look closely and you can see the planes up by the ceiling. The winning time was 14 seconds! *photo by Takuo Toda.*

Using the Runway

Now that you have a whole fleet of airplanes, you'll be wanting an airport. So here it is! There's a tarmac for parking planes, a hangar, a control tower, and of course the runway. It takes a bit of skill to land on it, but I'm sure you'll do great.

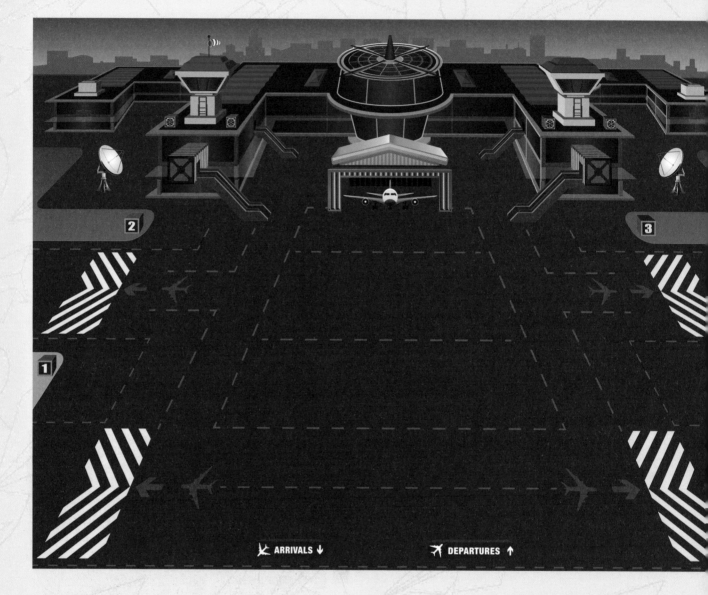

✈ ARRIVALS ↓   ✈ DEPARTURES ↑

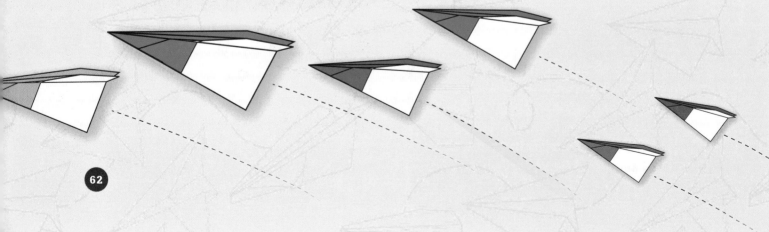

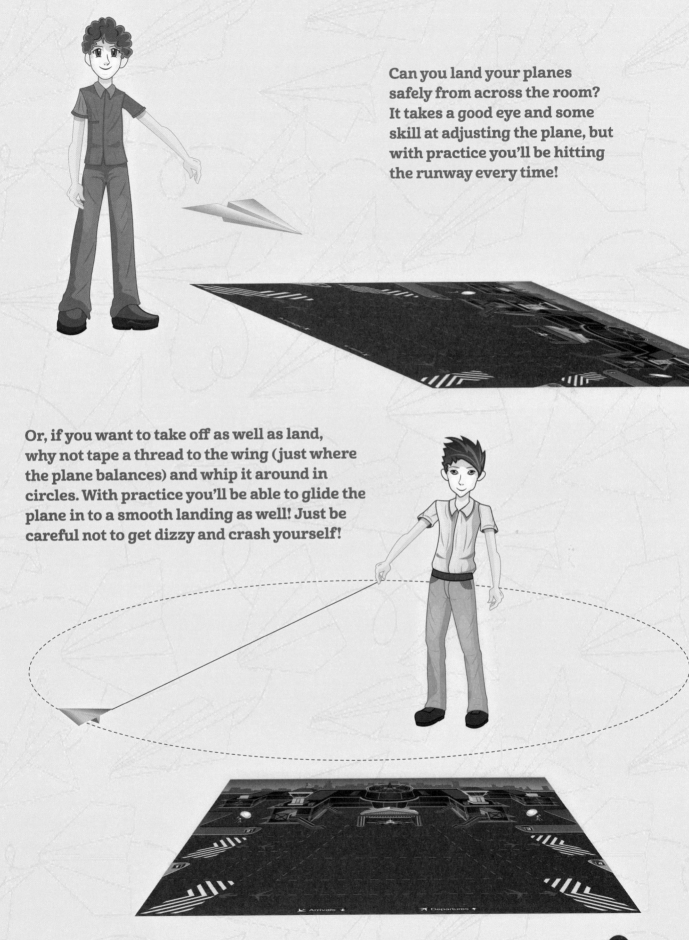

Can you land your planes safely from across the room? It takes a good eye and some skill at adjusting the plane, but with practice you'll be hitting the runway every time!

Or, if you want to take off as well as land, why not tape a thread to the wing (just where the plane balances) and whip it around in circles. With practice you'll be able to glide the plane in to a smooth landing as well! Just be careful not to get dizzy and crash yourself!

Published by Tuttle Publishing,
an imprint of Periplus Editions (HK) Ltd.

www.tuttlepublishing.com

Copyright © 2015 Andrew Dewar

ISBN 978-4-8053-1363-3

First Edition
26 25 24 23 22   16 15 14 13 12   2208VP
Printed in Malaysia

TUTTLE PUBLISHING® is a registered
trademark of Tuttle Publishing, a division
of Periplus Editions (HK) Ltd.

Distributed by:
North America, Latin America, and Europe
Tuttle Publishing
364 Innovation Drive
North Clarendon, VT 05759-9436 U.S.A.
Tel: (802) 773-8930 | Fax: (802) 773-6993
info@tuttlepublishing.com
www.tuttlepublishing.com

Japan and Korea
Tuttle Publishing
Yaekari Bldg., 3F
5-4-12 Osaki, Shinagawa-ku
Tokyo 141-0032
Tel: (81) 3 5437-0171 | Fax: (81) 3 5437-0755
sales@tuttle.co.jp
www.tuttle.co.jp

Asia Pacific
Berkeley Books Pte. Ltd.
3 Kallang Sector #04-01
Singapore 349278
Tel: (65) 6741-2178 | Fax: (65) 67414-2179
inquiries@periplus.com.sg
www.tuttlepublishing.com

"Books to Span the East and West"

Tuttle Publishing was founded in 1832 in the small New England town of Rutland, Vermont [USA]. Our core values remain as strong today as they were then—to publish best-in-class books which bring people together one page at a time. In 1948, we established a publishing office in Japan—and Tuttle is now a leader in publishing English-language books about the arts, languages and cultures of Asia. The world has become a much smaller place today and Asia's economic and cultural influence has grown. Yet the need for meaningful dialogue and information about this diverse region has never been greater. Over the past seven decades, Tuttle has published thousands of books on subjects ranging from martial arts and paper crafts to language learning and literature—and our talented authors, illustrators, designers and photographers have won many prestigious awards. We welcome you to explore the wealth of information available on Asia at **www.tuttlepublishing.com**.

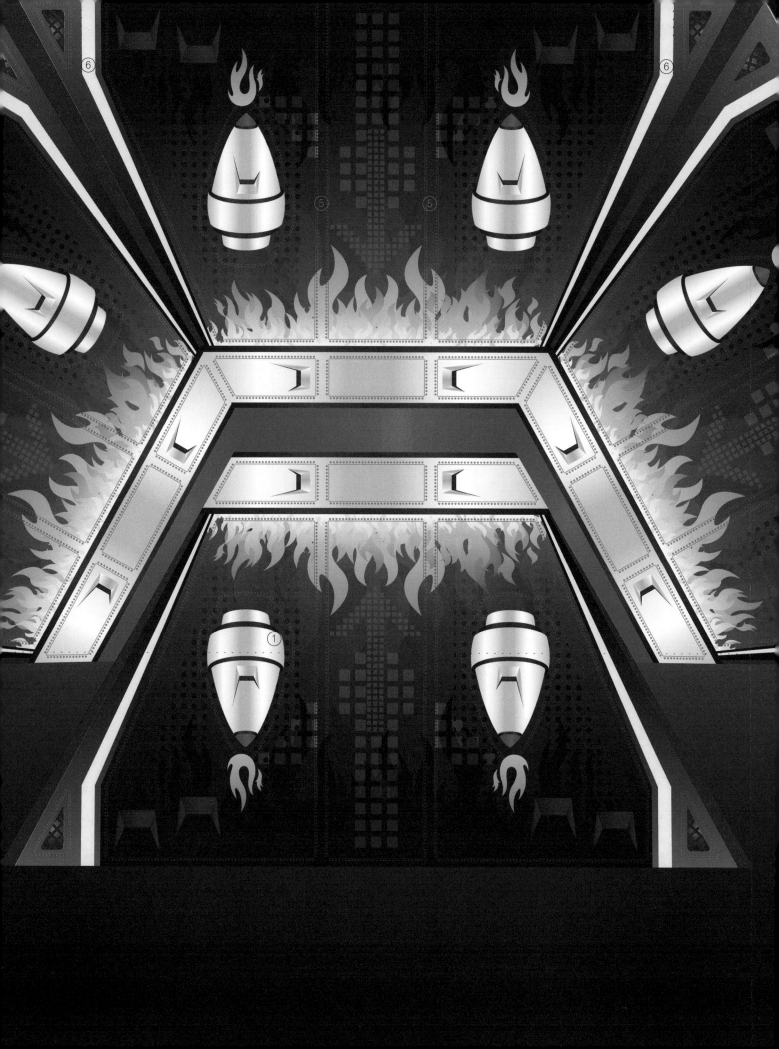

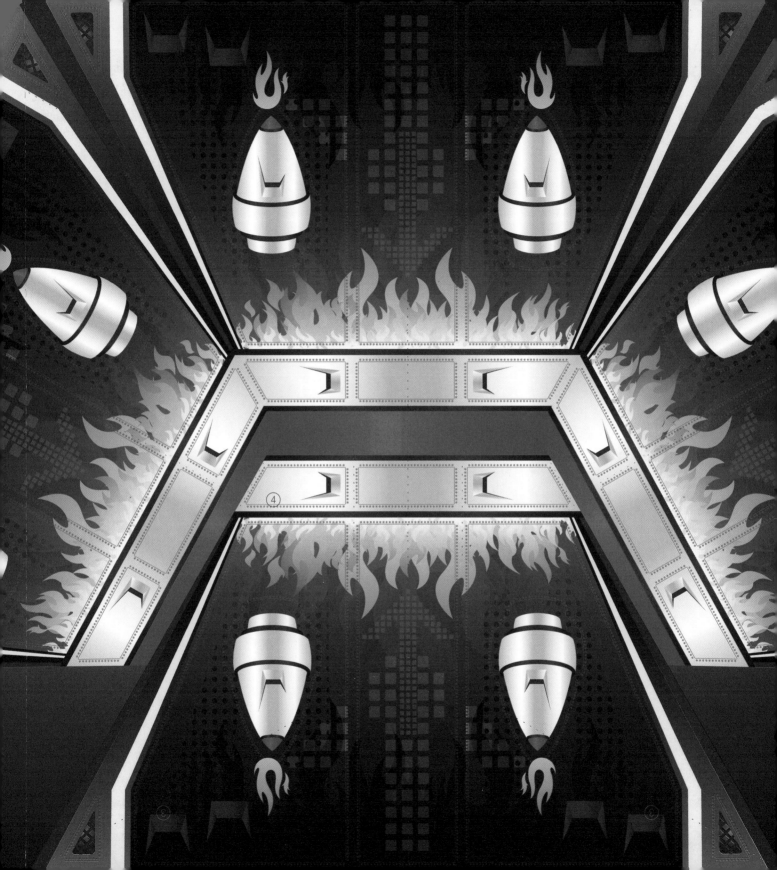

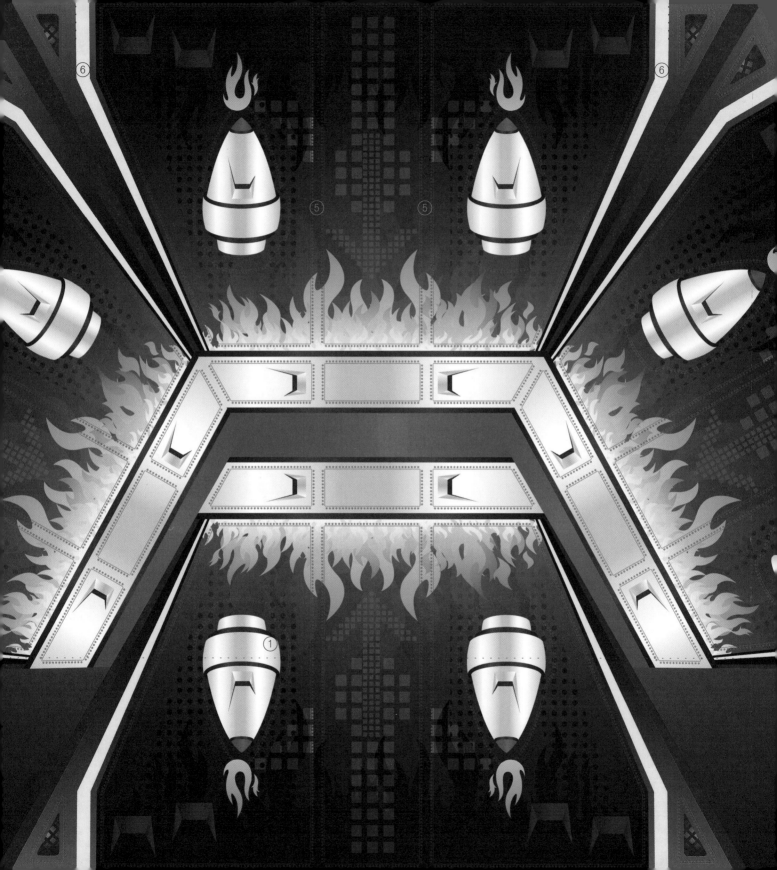

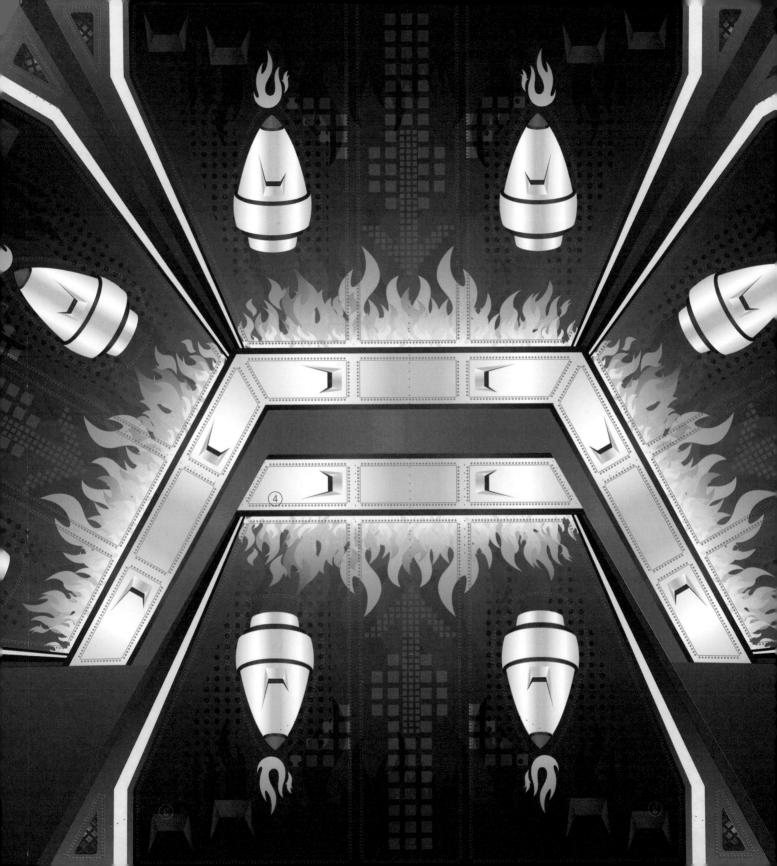

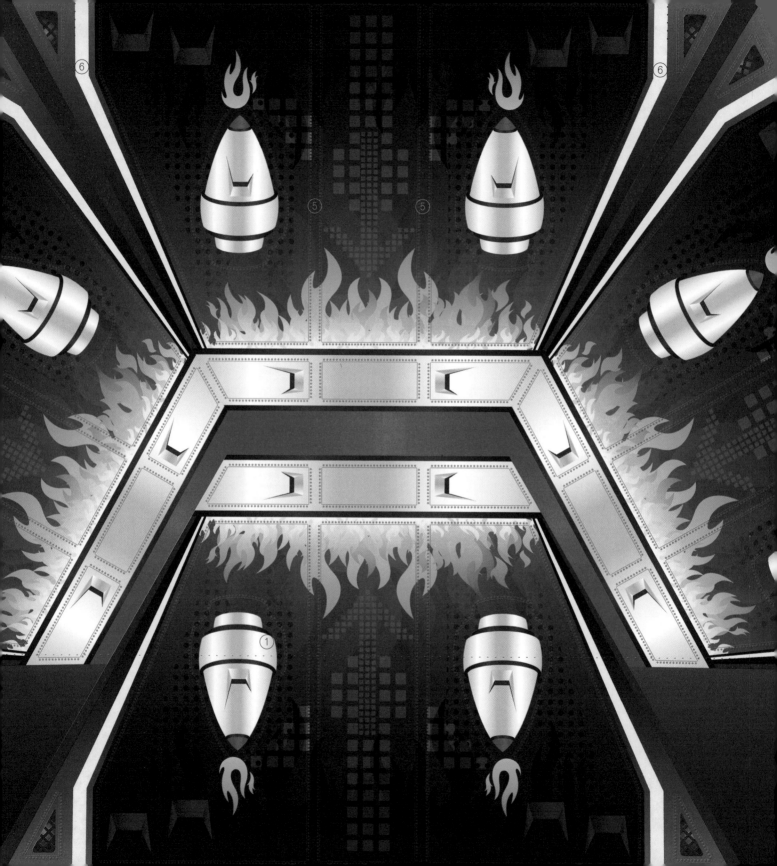

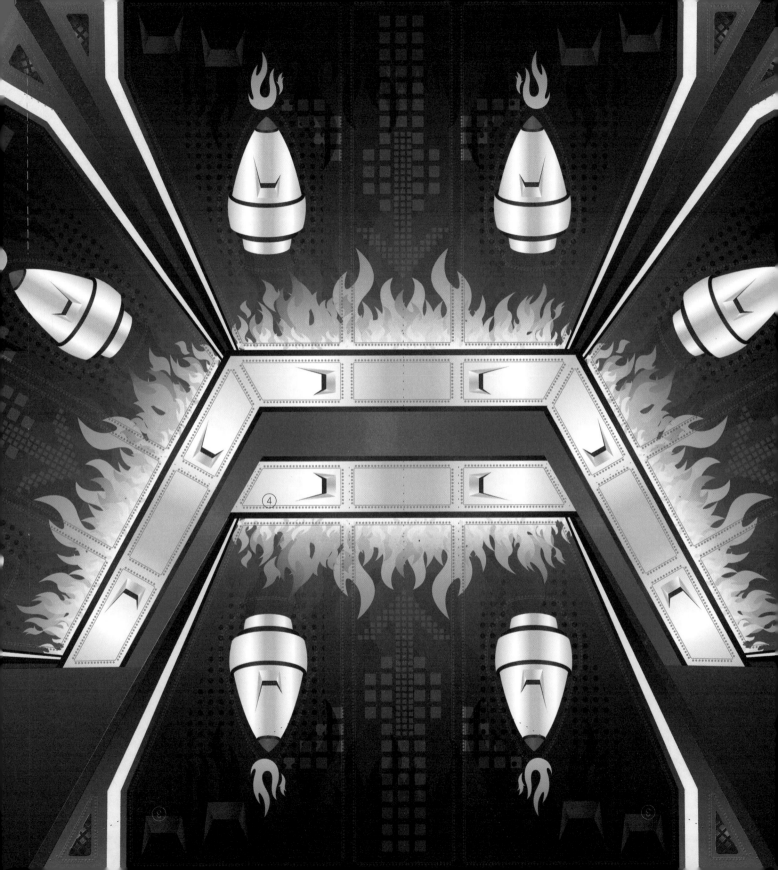

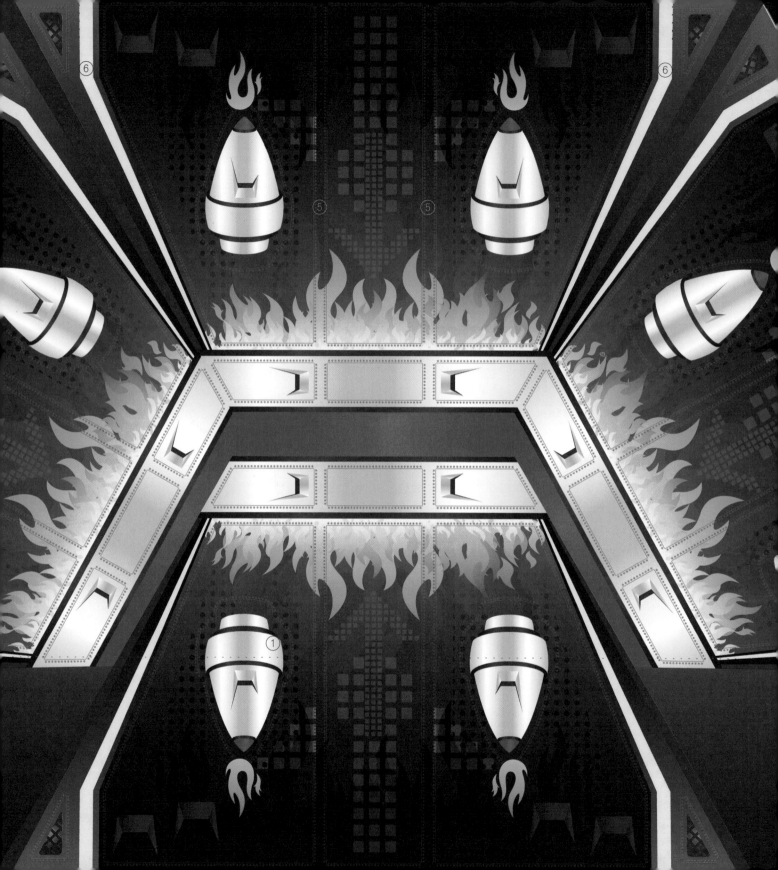

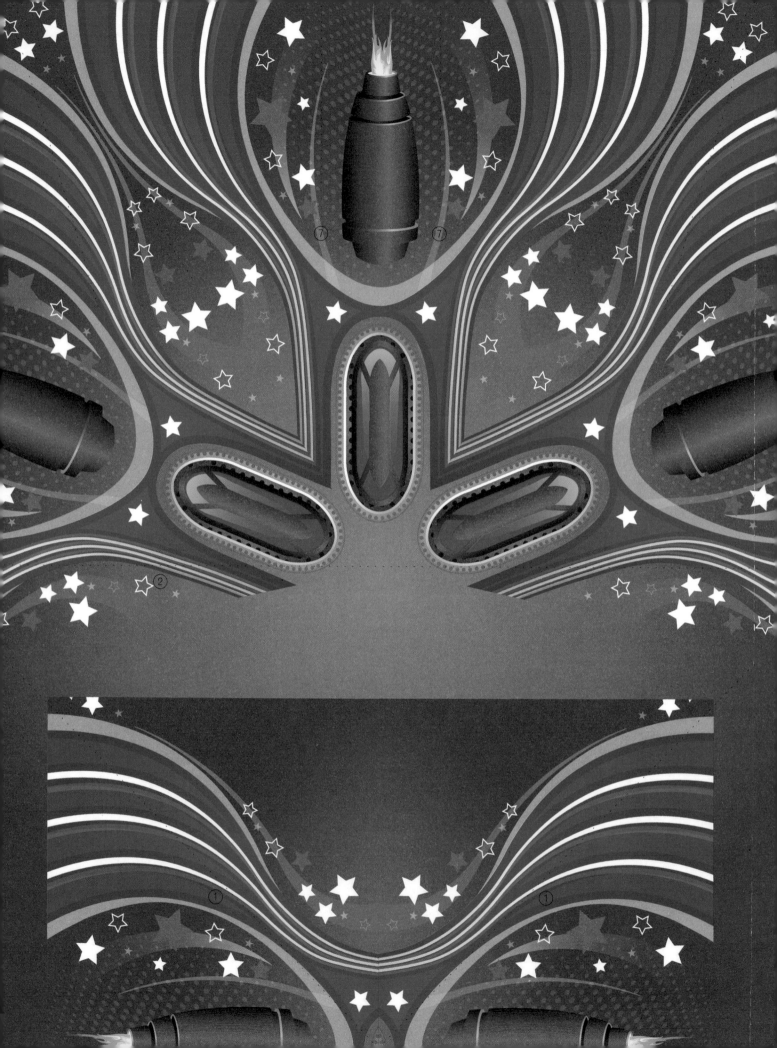

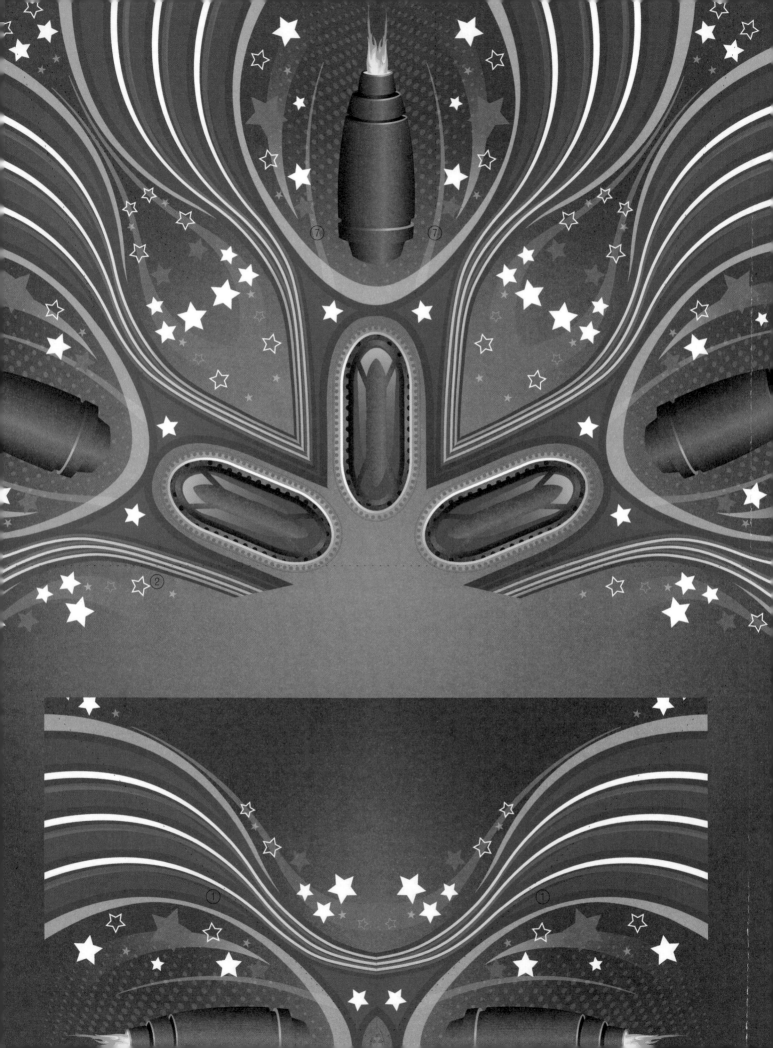

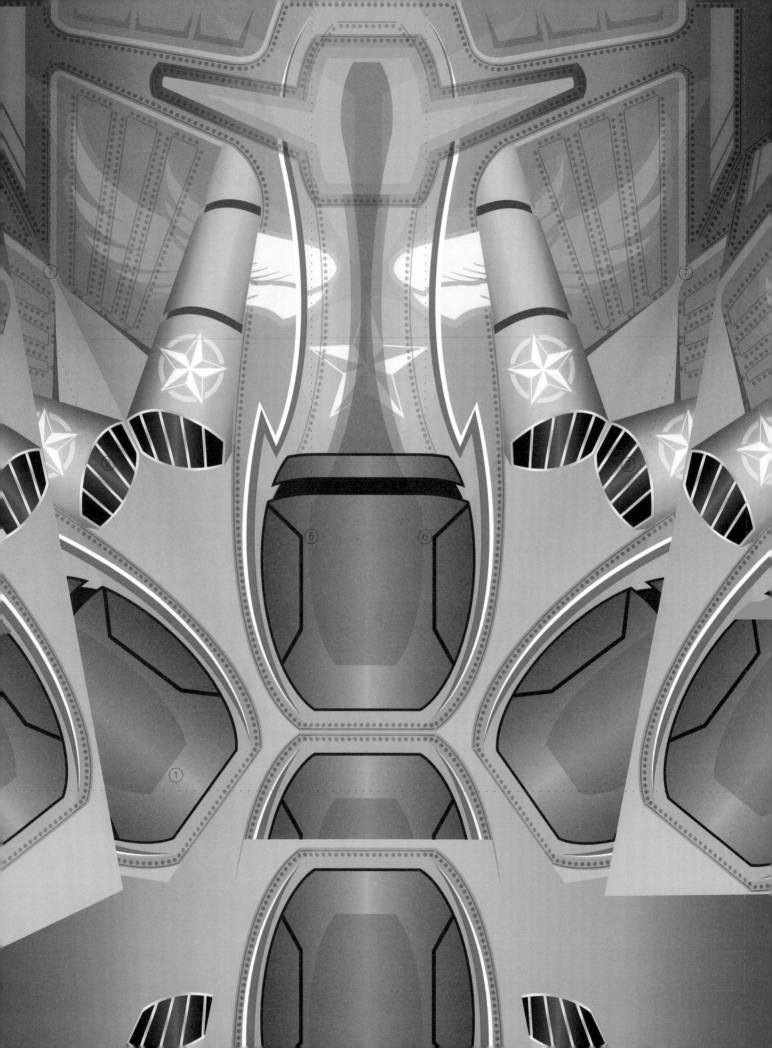

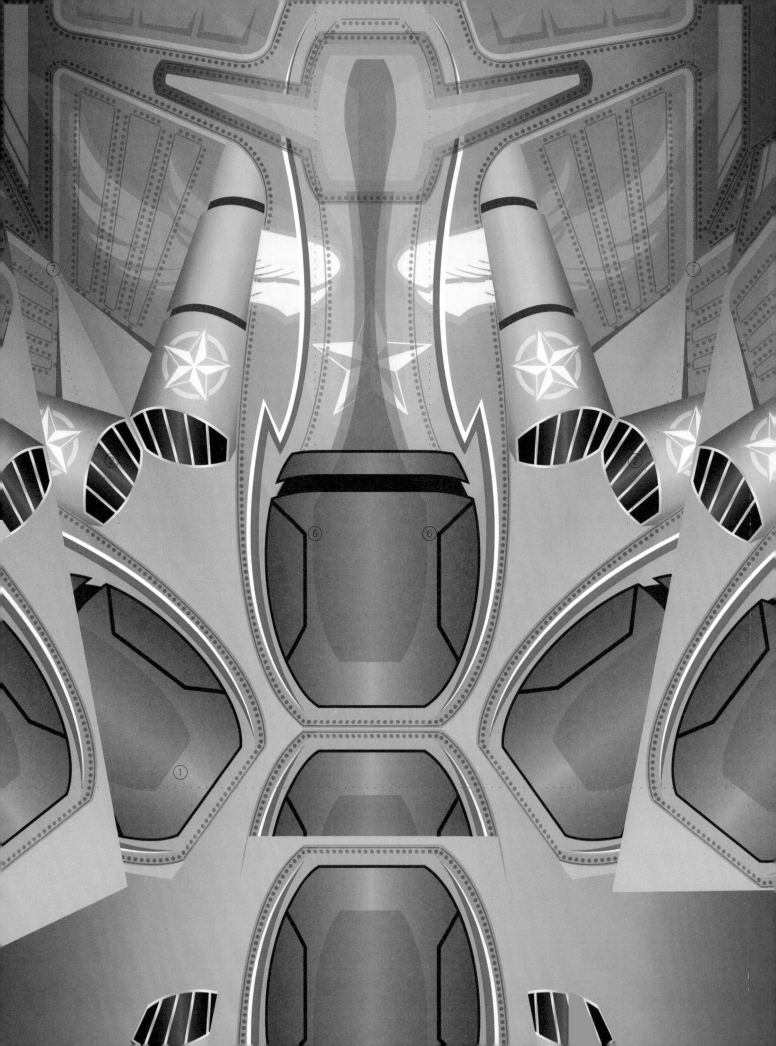

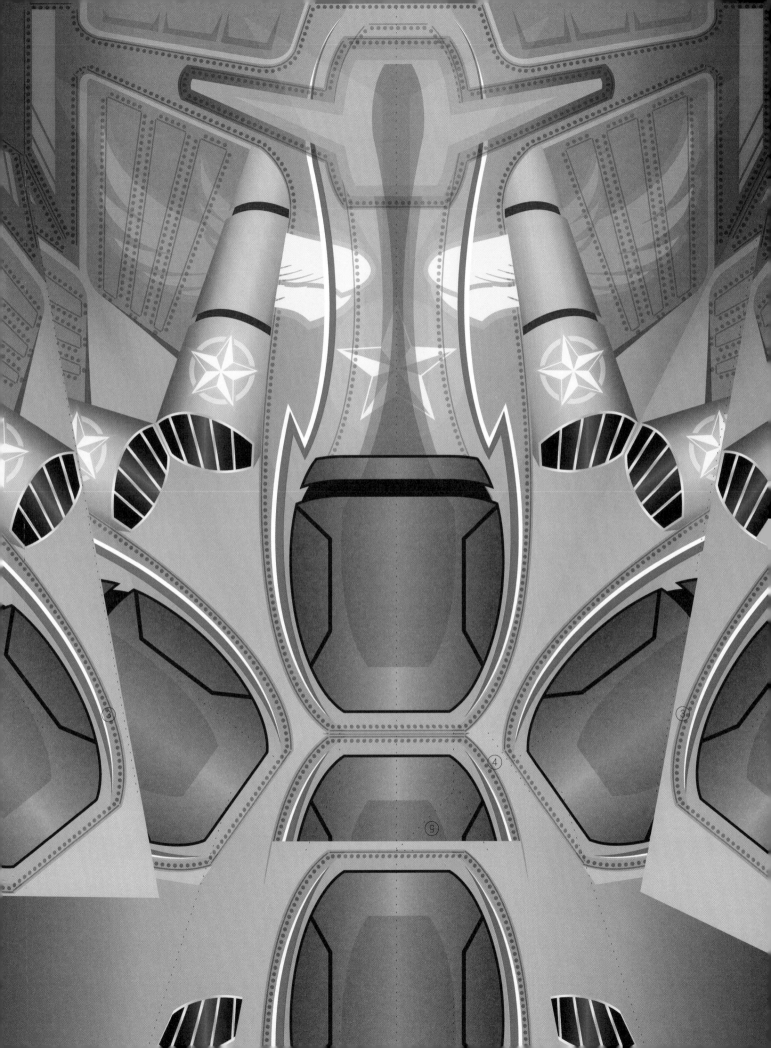

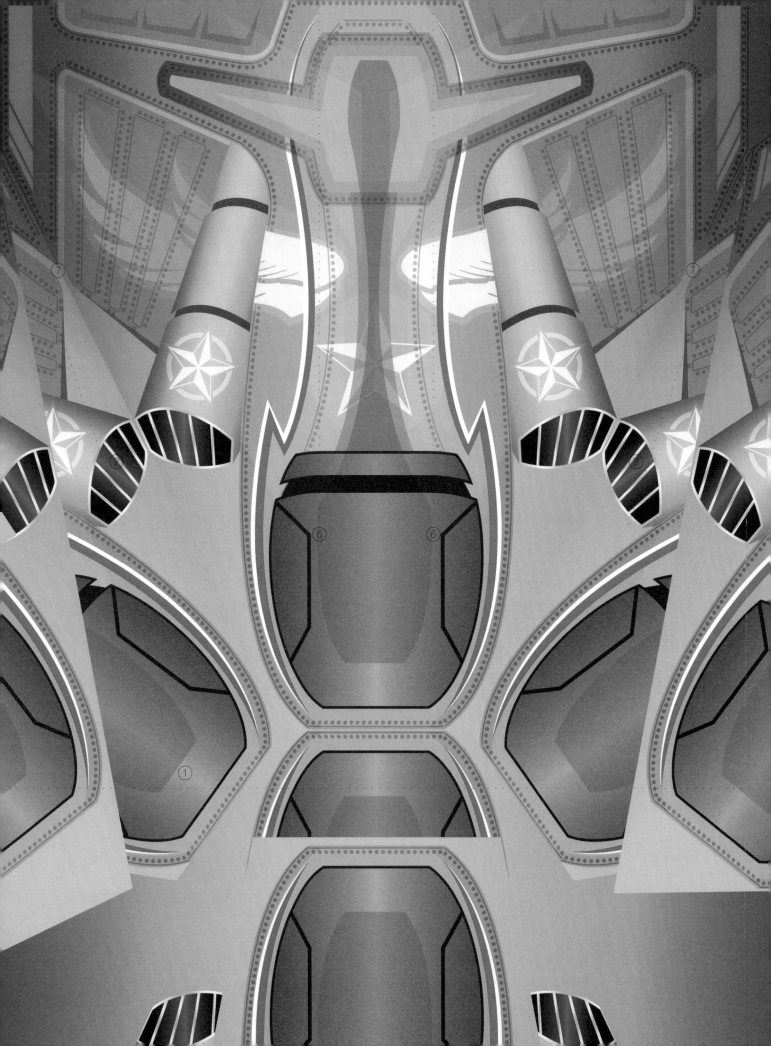

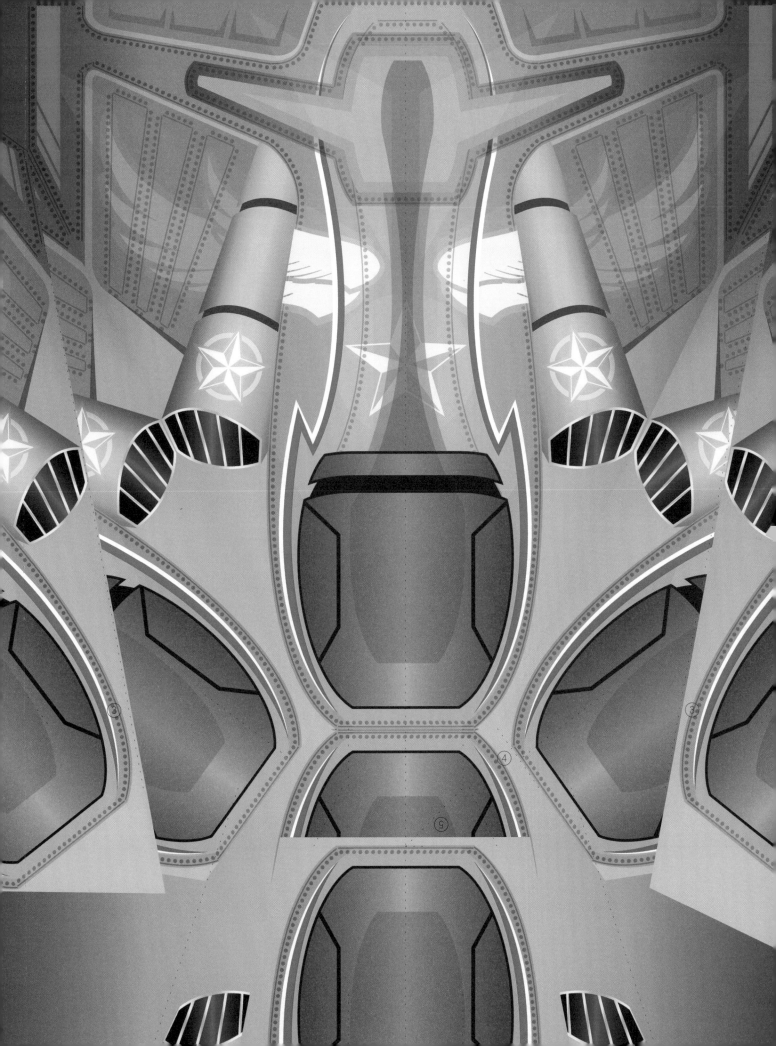

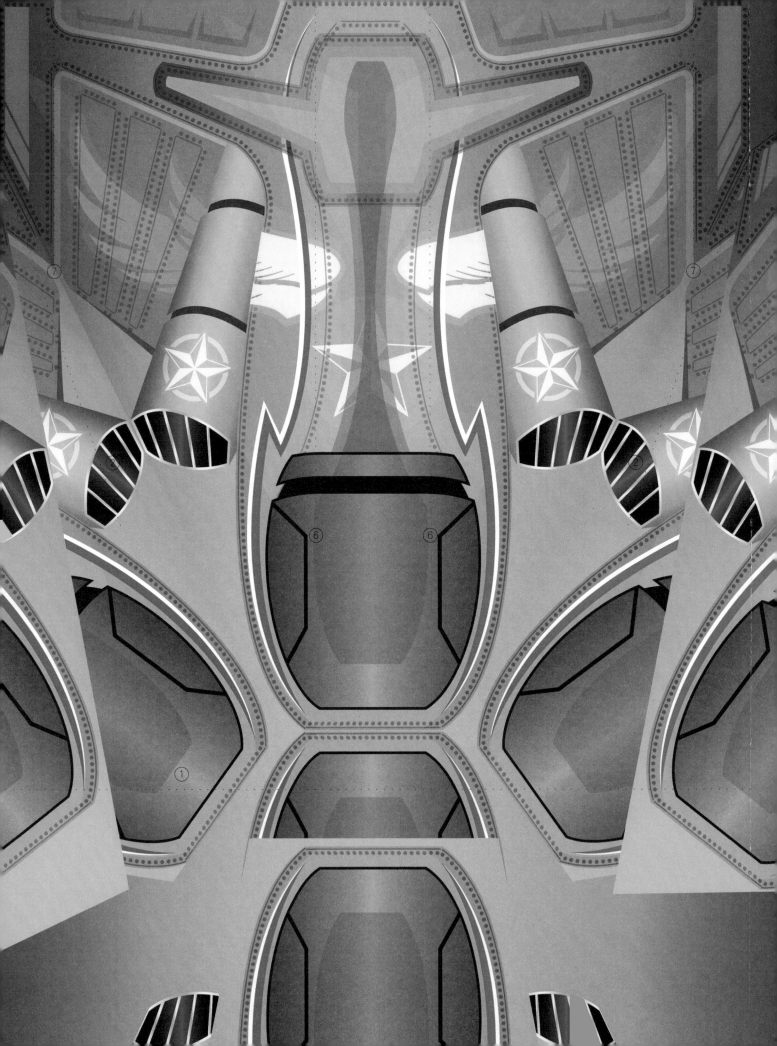